CYNGOR CAERDYDD
CARDIFF COUNCIL
LIBRARY SERVICE
WHITCHURCH
TEL: (029

D0256217

Glanmor Williams, 1920–2005.

A POCKET GUIDE

OWAIN GLYNDŴR

GLANMOR WILLIAMS

UNIVERSITY OF WALES PRESS
CARDIFF
1993

© Glanmor Williams, 1993
Reprinted 2005

All rights reserved. No part of this book may be reproduced, stored
in a retrieval system, or transmitted, in any form or by any means,
electronic, mechanical, photocopying, recording or otherwise,
without clearance from the University of Wales Press, 10 Columbus
Walk, Brigantine Place, Cardiff, CF10 4UP.
www.wales.ac.uk/press

British Library Cataloguing in Publication Data
A catalogue record for this book is available from the British Library.

ISBN 0-7083-1941-6

The right of Glanmor Williams to be identified as author of this
work has been asserted by her in accordance with sections 77 and
78 of the Copyright, Designs and Patents Act 1988.

Every effort has been made to contact the copyright holders of
material published in this volume but in the event of a query please
contact the publishers.

Printed in Malta by Gutenberg Press, Tarxien

For Huw

Contents

Illustrations

The plates are located between pages 49 and 50.

Preface

This book, first published by the Oxford University Press in 1966, was written at the request of my old and dearly-loved friend, the late Charles Mowat, then professor of history at the University College of North Wales, Bangor, as one of a series of Clarendon Biographies, edited by him and Miss M. R. Price. In this second edition, now being published by the University of Wales Press, it remains essentially what it was in 1966: a short, popular study of Owain Glyndŵr, one of the most remarkable and fascinating figures in the whole of Welsh history. In the last quarter of a century much has been written about him and his rebellion, notably by Professors R. R. Davies and R. A. Griffiths and Mr Rhidian Griffiths. I have taken the opportunity to incorporate much of the new material into this edition.

I have to thank Professors Davies and Griffiths not only for all the benefits I have derived from their published writings but also for their kindness in letting me read so much of their work before it appeared in print and for many enlightening conversations with them. I am indebted to the late Sir Idris Bell for his kind permission to quote on pages 7, 82 and 83 his translations of Welsh poetry, from *Dafydd ap Gwilym: Fifty Poems* (Honourable Society of Cymmrodorion, 1942) and the *Transactions* of the Cymmrodorion Society for 1940 and 1942. Similarly, I am grateful to the late Professor William Rees for allowing me to reproduce as the frontispiece to this volume the map from his *Historical Atlas of Wales* (Cardiff, 1951). My thanks go to Mr Peter White, Secretary of the Royal Commission on Ancient and Historical Monuments for Wales, who was extremely helpful in providing illustrations.

I should also like warmly to thank Ms Susan Jenkins and Mr Prys Davies for all the care and trouble they have shown in seeing the book through the press with their habitual kindness. My wife, as always, has been a tower of strength on whom I have been heavily dependent.

Swansea   Glanmor Williams
August, 1992

Acknowledgements

The author and publishers would like to thank the following for their kind permission to reproduce illustrations: © Crown Copyright: Royal Commission on the Ancient and Historical Monuments of Wales (Plates 1, 4, 5 and 6); Centre Historique des Archives Nationales, Paris (Plate 2); Clwyd-Powys Archaeological Trust (Plate 3); Joe Cocks Studio Collection © Shakespeare Birthplace Trust (Plate 7).

Glanmor Williams

Bu farw Syr Glanmor Williams ar 24 Chwefror 2005 tra oedd y gyfrol hon yn cael ei llywio drwy Wasg Prifysgol Cymru, gwasg a oedd mor agos at ei galon. Ef oedd yr hanesydd mwyaf a fagwyd erioed yng Nghymru. Er mai dyn bychan o gorff ydoedd, yr oedd yn gawr o ysgolhaig ac yn gymwynaswr mawr i'n cenedl. Ef oedd ein hawdurdod pennaf ar y cyfnod modern cynnar yng Nghymru, yn enwedig y Diwygiad Protestannaidd, a bydd ei lyfrau mawr, *The Welsh Church from Conquest to Reformation*, *Wales and the Reformation* a *Grym Tafodau Tân*, yn parhau tra bydd astudio ar hanes Cymru. Yr oedd rhychwant ei ddiddordebau yn eang a rhoes sylw arbennig i'r berthynas fywiol a chymhleth rhwng crefydd, llenyddiaeth a chenedligrwydd dros y canrifoedd. Tra oedd yn bennaeth Adran Hanes Prifysgol Cymru Abertawe rhwng 1957 a 1982 casglodd ynghyd nythaid disglair o haneswyr ifainc, a bu'r penodiadau hyn yn gwbl allweddol i ddatblygiad hanes Cymru dros yr hanner canrif diwethaf fel pwnc o fri rhyngwladol. Nid oedd ei debyg fel ysgogwr. Ef oedd symbylydd a golygydd cyntaf *Cylchgrawn Hanes Cymru*. Ef oedd golygydd cyffredinol y gyfres ysblennydd ar hanes sir Forgannwg a golygydd cyffredinol y gyfres safonol ar hanes Cymru a gyhoeddwyd ar y cyd gan Wasg Prifysgol Rhydychen a Gwasg Prifysgol Cymru. Bu'n ffigwr cyhoeddus eithriadol o ddylanwadol. Chwaraeodd ran amlwg yng ngweithgarwch ymron pob sefydliad diwylliannol cyhoeddus yng Nghymru, gan gynnwys Prifysgol Cymru, yr Amgueddfa Genedlaethol, Cyngor Celfyddydau Cymru, Comisiwn Brenhinol Henebion Cymru, Cyngor Adeiladau Hanesyddol Cymru, y Cyngor Darlledu a Llyfrgell Genedlaethol Cymru. Rhwng 1963 a 1965 yr oedd yn un o dri aelod Pwyllgor Hughes Parry a baratôdd adroddiad pellgyrhaeddol ei ddylanwad ar statws yr iaith Gymraeg. Ond hybu, astudio ac ysgrifennu am hanes Cymru oedd ei hoffter pennaf ac y mae'n anodd meddwl am hanesydd blaen-llaw yn y Gymru gyfoes sydd heb fod yn drwm yn ei ddyled. Yr oedd yn siaradwr bywiog a ffraeth, yn llawn straeon direidus am gymeriadau ein doe a'n heddiw. Er ei ddyrchafu'n farchog ym 1995, fel 'Glan' yr oedd pawb yn ei adnabod, ac ni wnaeth neb fwy nag ef i bontio'r bwlch rhwng yr hanesydd proff-esiynol meudwyaidd a'r lleygwr deallus. Yr oedd yn ŵr hael ei ysbryd, yn gyfaill agos-atoch, ac yn esiampl ardderchog i bob hanesydd ifanc. Chwith meddwl bod y 'bachgen bach' disglair o Ddowlais wedi ein gadael, a mawr yw ein diolch iddo am adael ar ei ôl y fath gnwd o lyfrau hanes godidog, gan gynnwys yr astudiaeth hon o un o wroniaid mwyaf cyfareddol Cymru.

Aberystwyth   Geraint H. Jenkins
2005

Glanmor Williams

Sir Glanmor Williams died on 24 February 2005 as this volume was making its way through the University of Wales Press, the publishing house he held so dear. He was the greatest historian ever raised in Wales. Although small in physical stature, he was an academic giant and a great benefactor to our nation. He was our foremost authority on the early modern period in Wales, especially the Protestant Reformation, and his substantial books, *The Welsh Church from Conquest to Reformation*, *Wales and the Reformation* and *Grym Tafodau Tân*, will endure as long as Welsh history remains a field of study. The range of his interests was extensive and he paid special attention to the lively and complex relationship between religion, literature and nationhood through the ages. During his time as head of the History Department at the University of Wales Swansea between 1957 and 1982 he gathered together a dis-tinguished array of young historians, and these appointments proved vital to the development of Welsh history as a subject of international renown over the last half century. He was a motivator par excellence. He was the instigator and first editor of the *Welsh History Review,* general editor of the splendid series on the history of Glamorgan, and general editor of the definitive series on the history of Wales published jointly by the Oxford University Press and the University of Wales Press. He was also an extremely influential public figure. He played a prominent part in the activities of nearly all the important public cultural institutions of Wales, including the University of Wales, the National Museum, the Arts Council of Wales, the Royal Commission on the Ancient and Historical Monuments of Wales, the Historic Buildings Council for Wales, the Broadcasting Council and the National Library of Wales. Between 1963 and 1965 he was one of the three members of the Hughes Parry Committee which compiled the influential and far-reaching report on the status of the Welsh language. But his main delight was promoting, studying and writing on Welsh history and it would be hard to name a leading historian in modern Wales who has not been heavily influenced by him. He was a lively and witty speaker, full of mischievous tales relating to characters from both our past and present. Although knighted in 1995, everyone knew him as 'Glan', and no one did more to bridge the gap between the hermitic professional historian and the intelligent layman. He was a generous-spirited man, a warm-hearted friend and an excellent model for any young historian. It is sad to think that this gifted 'little boy' from Dowlais has left us, and we are much indebted to him for bequeathing such a wealth of historical works, including this study of one of Wales's most charismatic heroes.

Aberystwyth   Geraint H. Jenkins
2005

1

Wales before Owain Glyndŵr

Och hyd atat ti, Dduw, na ddaw môr dros dir!
Pa beth y'n gedir i ohiriaw?

['0 God! that the sea might engulf the land,
why are we left to long-drawn weariness?']

Composed in the year 1283 by Gruffudd ab yr Ynad
Coch, these words of despair would have voiced the
feelings of many of the poet's compatriots that life
was no longer worth living. This bitter lament arose
from the death in battle of their prince, Llywelyn ap
Gruffudd (Llywelyn 'the Last'), in December 1282. Some
months later, Llywelyn's younger brother, Dafydd,
was captured and executed. With these men it seemed
that the independence of Wales had also died. The
Welsh people, however, were loath to accept the loss
of independence and, just over a century later in 1400,
they were to rise in rebellion under the last Welsh
ruler to proclaim himself prince of Wales. Owain
Glyndŵr – or as the English usually refer to him,
Owen Glendower – led the Welsh in their final, but
unsuccessful, bid to regain their independence.

Independence was dear to the Welsh because they
had enjoyed it for so long. Its origins went back to

the fifth century AD, when the eagle-standards of the Roman legions left Britain for good. During the following centuries, Anglo-Saxon rulers reigned in England, and Wales remained an independent country. Divided up into a number of small kingdoms, often at war with one another as well as with the Anglo-Saxons, it had its own kings, law, church, language, literature and culture. But this was to change following the Norman Conquest of England. William the Conqueror planted powerful Norman lords along the border between England and Wales and, within a few years, these lords began to thrust forward from bases like Chester, Shrewsbury, Hereford and Gloucester, along the river-valleys into the hilly heart of Wales. Taking advantage of the mobility of their own mounted knights and also of quarrels and divisions among the Welsh, they had, in a surprisingly short space of time, seized control of a large part of south and east Wales. They not only took over the land of Welsh rulers but also their powers, setting up new Norman lordships which were almost like little kingdoms of their own, practically independent of the king of England. In these lordships they built castles at strategic points like estuaries and river-crossings – wooden ones at first, later replaced by stone ones. To supply the needs of these castles, they created boroughs around them, and many of the oldest towns of Wales, for example, Chepstow, Cardiff, Brecon, Abergavenny, Neath, Swansea, Pembroke, and Cardigan, were first founded in this way. The Normans also brought in new methods of farming wherever the land was suitable for this. A lordship would often be divided into two parts, the Englishry and the Welshry. The Englishry was generally confined to low-lying areas around the castles and boroughs, and here the farming was usually manorial in its organization and the laws Anglo-Norman, with some mixture of Welsh custom. The Welshry lay in the more extensive upland districts, where the Welsh practised their own pastoral farming in kindred groups, living under Welsh law and custom. The whole area of Norman lordships was known as the March (march comes from a French word *marche* meaning frontier) or Marches of Wales.

The Normans' success in the March stirred some of the Welsh rulers to offer stiffer resistance to them. There were three areas in particular in which the Welsh fought back strongly in the twelfth and thirteenth centuries. In south-west Wales, roughly in the area of modern Carmarthenshire and Cardiganshire, the princes of Deheubarth stood fast. In the north-east, around modern Montgomeryshire and Denbighshire, the princes of Powys held their own. But much the most powerful and successful were the princes of Gwynedd in north-west Wales, firmly based on the mountain-strongholds of Snowdonia and the fertile granary of Anglesey. As rulers the princes of Gwynedd proved to be unusually apt pupils. They learnt both from their own experience and from the example of English kings such as Henry II (1154–89) or European rulers like Philip Augustus of France (1179–1223). They tried to unite lesser Welsh princes and chieftains under their own leadership and took full advantage of any temporary English weakness. The two greatest princes of Gwynedd, Llywelyn ab Iorwerth ('the Great', 1194–1240) and Llywelyn ap Gruffudd ('the Last', 1247–82), both of them fine soldiers, wise governors and clever diplomats, came very near to setting up a strong state covering the greater part of

Wales. Llywelyn ap Gruffudd was actually recognized as prince of Wales by Henry III (1216–72) in the Treaty of Montgomery of 1267. But in the person of King Edward I (1272–1307), Llywelyn found himself up against one of the strongest and most imperious of the English kings. The odds proved too great for even so determined and resourceful a leader as the Welsh prince. In the course of a desperate campaign against Edward he was killed in December 1282 and his brother Dafydd was executed at Shrewsbury in 1283. Thus died the last of the great princes of Gwynedd. The memory of their aims and ideals, however, lived long after them.

Edward I now took over the lands in north Wales previously held by the princes of Gwynedd and ruled them himself. To guard against any future uprising he built a number of powerful castles. These are among the finest to be seen anywhere in Europe and still stand, proud, formidable and largely intact, at places like Caernarfon or Conwy or Harlech. Around them he established boroughs, peopled by English traders and craftsmen and their families. He also brought in some English law and ways of government. He divided Gwynedd into the three shires of Anglesey, Caernarfon and Merioneth, and appointed the same kind of officers to govern them – sheriffs and coroners – as English shires had. For purposes of justice and finance he grouped the three shires together and put two major officers, the Justiciar and the Chamberlain, in charge of these aspects of their government. These shires, together with the county of Flint in north-east Wales and Cardiganshire and Carmarthenshire in south-west Wales, made up that part of royally-ruled Wales which became known as the Principality. Later on, in 1301, Edward I created his eldest son prince of Wales and put the Principality in his charge. This was the first of a line of twenty-one eldest sons of the sovereign of England (including the present prince) who have held the title of prince of Wales.

Edward's conquest, however, did not give him any more real authority over the March of Wales. It might perhaps have been better for Wales if it had. Edward needed the help of the warrior-lords of the March for his wars in France and Scotland, and although he tried to keep a firm hand on them, he hesitated to press them too hard and he was actually obliged to create some new lordships after his conquest. He was followed by weaker rulers like Edward II (1307–27) or Richard II (1377–99), who found it much more difficult to curb the lords of the March. So for 250 years, from 1284 to 1536, Wales remained divided into two parts, Principality and March, with the March itself still further divided into a number of separate lordships.

In some ways Edward's plans for Wales worked well. Though Welshmen were not at first trusted to hold the highest posts in the government of their country, many of the leading families of *uchelwyr* or gentlemen held positions at a lower level within their own areas. They worked closely with the king's officers, and in time a few of the most favoured and trusted of them were allowed to hold quite high office themselves or to act as deputies for absentee English officers, like Sir Gruffudd Llwyd (d. 1335) who was sheriff of Caernarfonshire (1301–5, 1308–10), Anglesey (1305–6) and Merioneth (1314–16, 1321–7). The king also found that he could recruit many Welshmen as soldiers for his frequent wars in Scotland and France. The speciality of the Welsh was their outstanding skill as archers, for they used the longbow better than anyone else at this time. We find Welsh archers serving in the English army at the battle of Falkirk as early as 1298, and from then onwards they were found in large numbers in the English armies of the fourteenth century. They shared prominently in such famous victories as the battles of Creçy (1346) and Poitiers (1356). The Red Dragon of Cadwaladr, a Welsh hero of the seventh century, became the recognized emblem of the Welsh, and at Creçy, when the Black Prince was thrown from his horse, it was the dragon–banner of Wales that was flung over him in protection while his enemies were beaten off. It was probably at Creçy, too, that the leek became the Welshman's special badge when Welshmen plucked leeks and wore them in their helmets.

Very sensibly, Edward I did not try to prevent the Welsh gentlemen or soldiers from speaking their own language. Nor did he suppress Welsh literature. Hitherto, Welsh poets and writers had depended chiefly on the independent Welsh princes for support. After the Conquest they attached themselves to the households of the *uchelwyr*, who were themselves often descended from the former princely families. In this period Welsh literature flourished as it has rarely done, before or since. The greatest poet Wales ever produced and one of Europe's finest medieval poets, Dafydd ap Gwilym (flourished 1340–70), now appeared on the scene. It is interesting to note that he was descended from a Welsh family closely associated with English government in Wales. From his and other poets' verses we derive an attractive picture of some aspects of the life led by their patrons among the *uchelwyr*. He found Owain Glyndŵr's own province of Powys to be

> Powys the bounteous and benign
> With her fair taverns and flowing wine,
> An orchard where all joyance grew.

And all over Wales he opened men's eyes to the beauty of their land:

> Every oak's high summit rings
> With the young bird's lusty carollings,
> And every copse is sweet with song,
> And cuckoo calls, and the days are long,
> And a white haze, when the wind dies,
> Over the heart of the valley lies,
> And evening skies are blue and clear,
> And the trees ashimmer with gossamer.

His verse shows us a gay, lively, energetic people with a zest for life and a sparkling sense of humour. There was nothing drab or downtrodden about this.

But there was another and darker side to the picture. The changes introduced by Edward I sometimes caused real difficulty and discontent. Much would depend on the spirit in which the king's chief officials in Wales, not themselves Welsh, would approach their task. All too often they carried out their duties in harsh and unsympathetic fashion, treating Wales as a colony to be ruled for the king's profit and their own, in the interests of the English minority and not those of the Welsh people. Soon after the conquest whole Welsh communities were moved from good lands to poorer ones in order to make room for English settlers. In addition, English laws were frequently strongly disliked in Wales, especially when they applied to land. Welsh land law paid greater respect to the rights of the whole group of kinsmen than English law, and the Welsh tended bitterly to resent changes which they thought deprived them of their proper rights to land which gave them their living. For example, under Welsh law when a Welsh freeholder died without heirs, his land would be divided among his relatives, but under English law it might pass into the hands of the king who would not necessarily decide to grant it to the dead man's kinsmen. Nor did the Welsh relish having to find a good deal more ready money in order to pay heavier English taxes. They found this all the more burdensome because the only way they could raise money was by selling their produce in the boroughs peopled by English traders – they were forbidden to trade anywhere else. None of these practices endeared English rule to the Welsh. They could, on occasion, lead to severe outbreaks of violence, such as occurred in 1345, when a leading royal official, Henry Shaldeforde, was set upon by Welshmen and murdered.

The Welsh were a proud people who would, at best, have found it hard to accept the idea of being a conquered race. They often consoled themselves with the memory of ancient prophecies which, handed down from generation to generation by the poets, had been immensely popular for centuries past. An English chronicler explains the hold of the prophecies thus:

The Welsh habit of revolt against the English is an old-standing madness . . . And this is the reason. The Welsh, formerly called Britons, were once noble crowned over the whole realm of England; but they were expelled by the Saxons and lost both the name and the kingdom. The fertile plains went to the Saxons; but the sterile and

mountainous districts to the Welsh. But from the sayings
of the prophet Merlin they still hope to recover England.
Hence it is that the Welsh frequently rebel, hoping to
give effect to the prophecy.

It was the bards who, above all, preserved these traditions. They transmitted them to the sons of the
uchelwyr, of whom they were the teachers, and, travel-
ling from noble household to household, they kept
the old hopes alive as they retold the ancient prophecies around the blazing hearth or the banqueting
board on long dark winter evenings.

Quite apart from any friction between Welsh and
English, however, the hundred years or so which followed Edward I's conquest of Wales were likely to
have been a time of great difficulty and distress. All
over Europe, in an age when the great majority of
people earned their living on the land, the demand for
farm products decreased and the price of the produce
tended to fall. As a result, trade was less prosperous,
many peasants became poorer, and the area of land
they thought it worth cultivating or the amount of
food worth producing for sale became smaller. It also
seems likely that the climate deteriorated in this period,
and the appalling famines experienced from 1315 to
1317 were only the first of many periods of dearth.
Conditions were made worse by prolonged wars. The
year 1337 saw the opening of the Hundred Years War
between England and France, which gave rise to
heavy, frequent and unpopular taxes, shortages of
coin, and enforced devaluation. Then in 1348–50
came the Black Death, the first and worst attack of a
dreadful plague which killed off from one-third to
one-half of the population. The first outbreak was

followed by a whole series of later ones at intervals of about twelve to fifteen years. The effect of these plagues, in general, was to make trade and agriculture still more difficult. They led to a further falling off in demand, and often left towns and country districts with a population too reduced in size and strength to be able to continue producing as efficiently as they had done before the plague. They also had the effect of lowering people's morale and confidence, making them depressed and frightened. Even the Church suffered badly by the end of the fourteenth century and lost much of the respect and devotion which men had earlier shown it. Of course, there were a minority who managed to do quite well out of all these troubles. In any age, no matter how distressed it may be, there are always some who are either lucky or quick-witted or unscrupulous enough to rise to the top. But the majority had found life getting steadily harder, and they were restless and discontented. No wonder that by the 1390s many thought that the end of the world was about to come and that the year 1400 would be the last in human history.

These generally unsettled conditions prevailed in Wales too. If anything, it was in a worse plight than many other parts of Europe for, as far as soil and climate went, it was a poor country in which farming was never easy, and it had felt severely the pinch of growing pressures already mentioned – famine, war, plague, and slump. But though times had become so hard, the rulers of the Principality and the March had not eased up on their demands. On the contrary, in order to keep up the amount of revenue coming in to them, the king's officials in the Principality and the lords' officers in the March had squeezed the populace even more tightly than usual. All classes in Wales had felt the pressure. At the bottom of the scale were the labourers. It is true that, because the many deaths caused by plague had made labourers scarce, their wages had gone up, but even so, most of them were still desperately poor and miserable, and many had to wander back and forth into England to find what work they could. Just above the labourers came the unfree peasants or serfs. They were pressed extremely hard by their lords and suffered very grievously as the result of plague. Consequently, from time to time large numbers of them simply fled from their scanty holdings to join the growing army of landless and discontented labourers or the poorest classes in the towns. Even the better-off free men found it too much of an effort to hold their own in face of reduced numbers, heavy demands for money from king and lord, and hard times in farming. Not a few of them had to sell their lands to richer or more powerful neighbours, while others struggled on with a growing sense of despair. Amongst all these groups there were plenty of families and individuals who had good reason to feel angry and rebellious.

But whether they would rebel or not depended chiefly on the attitude of the men who were their natural leaders, the *uchelwyr*. These descendants of the former princes and chieftains still exercised a tremendous amount of authority and influence over their compatriots. As long as they remained more or less loyal to the king and the lords of the March there was not much danger of a serious uprising. On the whole they had probably suffered less from the crises of the age than any other group of Welsh people.

Very often, indeed, they and the more fortunate free peasants had been able to take advantage of their poorer neighbours' misfortunes to add to their own possessions. They had also, as we have seen, acted as officials for the king and the lords of the March. But some of these men, too, were becoming increasingly restless during the last quarter of the fourteenth century. The wars with France, in which many of them had done well out of plunder and ransom earlier in the century, were now going very badly. Furthermore, even *uchelwyr* could not entirely escape the burdensome taxes, levies and fines that were being raised from rich and poor alike, in order to keep up the income of king and lord. What was more, during the reign of Richard II there was a growing tendency to cut them out from holding important positions in the Principality and the March. Nor could they easily hope to improve their lot by settling in the boroughs, for the inhabitants of the English boroughs in the Principality were loud in their demands that the Welsh should be kept out. From the March and the neighbouring English counties there came bitter complaints in almost every Parliament that sat between 1378 and 1400 against ambitious Welshmen who bought land there or settled in the towns, together with demands that they should be sternly dealt with in England and Wales. English merchants from these same areas complained that they were being unjustly dealt with in the Welsh Marches and demanded that a check be placed on Welsh officers there.

Brothers and friends of the *uchelwyr* who entered the Church formed an influential group of educated men, and they, too, had their grievances. During the last quarter of the fourteenth century they had been finding themselves more and more shut out of the highest and wealthiest livings in the Welsh Church. It had become almost impossible for a Welshman to be made a bishop in Wales unless he could get the pope to intervene on his behalf, and the pope rarely wished to offend the king. Whereas earlier in the Middle Ages it had been usual for Welshmen or men born in Wales to be made bishops of Welsh dioceses, between 1372 and 1400, out of a total of sixteen bishops appointed in Wales, only one was a Welshman. Many of the other most valuable offices in the Church were similarly going to Englishmen who were servants of the king or Marcher lords. At the University of Oxford, where many young Welshmen intent upon entering the Church went for their education, they sometimes found a very hostile atmosphere. In 1395, there was an ugly riot in which the cry of 'Slay, slay the Welsh dogs' was raised in the streets. In fairness, it ought to be added that the Welsh (and Irish) students were a violent and hot-tempered company, frequently bent on making trouble themselves.

All this suggests a rising undercurrent of hostility between Welsh and English during the last quarter of the fourteenth century. The outlook even for the Welsh *uchelwyr* was distinctly bleaker. Up until now, most of them had been prepared to cooperate with the English government. But they did so always on condition that their rights and interests were respected and safeguarded. They were, all the same, a proud and high-spirited group, often with considerable experience of warfare and leadership in the armies of the king and the lords. If they became convinced that the English authorities were no longer willing to accord them the position they had previously enjoyed they might very well decide to fight for their rights. And they were equipped to do so; for each of them had at his beck and call his *plaid* or retinue of supporters, bound to him by ties of blood or tenancy or money or fear, or a mixture of all or any of them. The *plaid* of Rhys and Gwilym ap Tudur, for instance, has been examined in detail and been shown to have con-sisted of men of some substance but willing to resort to violence. They were a closely-knit band of adven-turers devoted to their leaders before and after 1400. If men like the Tudur brothers raised the flag of revolt they would certainly be followed by many lesser figures who had grievances enough of their own. Any military trouble they might create in Wales would be all the more serious for England because of the probability that her customary foes, France and Scotland, might be eager to exploit it to their own advantage. They had already shown their eagerness to do so more than once in the fourteenth century (France, 1339, 1346 and 1359; and Scotland, 1315–17, 1325–7,1335 and 1339).

It was at critical junctures like these, when they lost confidence in the goodwill of king and lord, that the *uchelwyr* and others began to listen more intently to the siren-songs of the bards who pro-claimed the coming of a Welsh deliverer. Already in 1370–2 the English government in Wales had had cause to be seriously alarmed by the claims of Owain Lawgoch ('Owen of the Red Hand', died 1378). Owain was a descendant of the princes of Gwynedd who had taken service in the armies of the king of France. He had declared himself to be the true prince of Wales, 'through the power of succession, through my lineage, and through my right as the descendant of my forefathers the kings of that country'. He proclaimed his intention of returning to claim his rightful inheritance and lead his people. If he had landed he might have made a great impact; in fact he was killed by treachery before he could do so. But for a time there was a real danger that he might invade Wales and meet with wide support. After his death neither his name nor his cause was forgotten. Some poets suggested that another Owain would emerge to take his place. If a man who could really claim to be a prince of ancient Welsh blood did indeed step forward, his call to arms might, in the disturbed state of Wales in 1400, be answered by a multitude of his countrymen. There were now many among them who echoed in their hearts the longing of a leading poet Iolo Goch, who sang:

> Many a time have I desired
> To see a lord of our kin.

It was an *uchelwr* sprung from a princely house who had often rewarded Iolo for his poetry who was now to offer himself as such a lord. He was Owain Glyndŵr.

2

Owain Glyndŵr before the Rebellion

Who was this Owain who set himself up as a leader in 1400? On both sides of his family he could claim to be descended from Welsh princes. His father's family was sprung from the former princes of Powys in north-east Wales. Since the time of Edward I's conquest, the family had managed to cling to some fragments of their once-extensive lands. What was left to them they now held from the king of England in much the same way as did the other barons of the March, almost all of whom were not Welsh. But in the eyes of the Welsh, Owain's descent from princes made him infinitely more noble than the other barons. The prominent poet, Iolo Goch, saw it in this light:

> Owain is a baron whose lineage I know,
> never was there a truer lord.
> Worthless is any baron
> unless he be sprung from the same stock as he.

The family's estates now consisted of the two lordships of Glyndyfrdwy and Cynllaith. Glyndyfrdwy, or the

'Glen of the Water of Dee', lay in the narrow gorge of the River Dee between Llangollen and Corwen. It was this beautiful but rather wild region of heath and woodland which gave Owain the name by which he became famous: Owain Glyndŵr ('Owen of the Glen of Water') or in its English form Owen Glendower. The second lordship, Cynllaith Owain, lay on the other side of the Berwyn Mountains from Glyndyfrdwy and was a more fertile and cultivated area. Here stood the family's chief residence at Sycharth, of which no traces now remain except the motte or mound on which it stood. It was destroyed by Prince Henry (later Henry V) in a punitive raid of 1403 and was never rebuilt. Not a great deal is known about Owain's father, Gruffudd, who died when still a young man, or of his immediate ancestors. They had been content to live a quiet life as country squires and had played no very outstanding part in the history of Wales. Earlier princes of Powys through-out the Middle Ages had found themselves in an unenviable situation. They were pressed between the princes of Gwynedd, whom they envied and mis-trusted, and the kings of England, whom they feared and tried to placate. Some celebrated leaders had come from their midst, but of all the Welsh princes they had perhaps played the least heroic role. Certainly, they had not given much sign that from their stock would ultimately come the greatest national hero of Wales.

Owain's mother, Elen, also came from a royal family. She was descended from the princes of Deheubarth in south Wales. From her, Owain inherited land in south Cardiganshire and, what was more important, a claim to the possible loyalty and support of the men of the south. He could also claim to be related to the line of the great princes of Gwynedd, Gruffudd ap Cynan (1075–1137) and Owain Gwynedd (1147–80). After the death of Owain Lawgoch in 1378, therefore, he could present himself as heir to the heritage of the two Llywelyns, whose arms – the four lions of Gwynedd – he was to assume in the course of his rebellion.

Owain's Family Tree

Madog ap Gruffudd (d. 1236), prince of Northern Powys

Gruffudd Maelor (d. 1269)

Madog   Llywelyn   Owain   Gruffudd Fychan (d. 1289)

Madog ap Gruffudd (d. 1304)

Gruffudd ap Madog (d. 1343)

Gruffudd Fychan
(d. before 1370) married
Elen daughter of Owain ap
Thomas Llywelyn

Owain Glyndŵr =
Margaret Hanmer

There was a strong tradition that he was born in his mother's ancestral home in south Wales when she was on a visit to her family there; but this seems very unlikely. The chances are that he was born at his father's chief residence in the lordship of Cynllaith. This was at Sycharth in the parish of Llansilin.

If we cannot tell for certain where Owain was born, neither do we know definitely when that happened either. Three possible dates are given for the year of his birth: 1349, 1354, and 1359. The year 1349 derives from a persistent tradition that he was born in the year of the great plague, the Black Death. The second date is the remarkably precise one of 28 May 1354, taken by the celebrated antiquary Thomas Pennant (1726–98) from an ancient manuscript used by him. But the safest source is the record of a trial of 1386 in which Owain Glyndŵr acted as a witness (see below p. 22) and it declares that he was then 'twenty-seven years and more'. Of the details of his early life we know very little but some interesting new facts concerning him have come to light in recent years.

We now know that his father died before 1370 and that Owain had the cares of landownership thrust upon him much sooner than used to be supposed. This is proved by a document noting debts that were outstanding to Richard Fitzalan (d. 1376), earl of Arundel, from Michaelmas 1370 to Michaelmas 1371. It records a debt of thirty marks owed by Owain's mother, Elen, described as widow of 'Gruff. de Glindorde', to the earl. The fact that she borrowed money from him suggests that he knew her personally and, through her, her son. She may, indeed, have entrusted the boy to the nearby household of the Arundels, who were lords of Chirk and Dinas Brân, as an eminently suitable place in which to be trained in 'manly skills and polite manners'.

Owain was also sent to London at some point to acquire an education to fit him for his place in the world. A Latin chronicler tells us that he was sent 'to be an apprentice of the law at Westminster' – possibly under the tuition of his future father-in-law, the eminent lawyer Sir David Hanmer. Here, at the Inns of Court he may have spent as long as seven years. This was a most valuable training for a young man. The Inns of Court were a place where not only men who wanted to be professional lawyers went to be trained. They were also rather like a public school for the sons of the best families. There they learned a good deal about the law and government and also how to behave in the best society.

From being a law student Owain turned to complete his education by becoming a squire and soldier. The way for a young man of good birth to do so was to enter the service of one of the greatest lords of the kingdom. The latter liked to have around them a body of high-spirited retainers to act as their lieutenants in battle and tournament and to uphold their dignity in all the other colourful ceremonies of courtly life and chivalry. The poet Gruffudd Llwyd, who was perhaps attached to Owain's household, describes him as 'resplendent in gold and scarlet trappings of the finest kind', 'fighting in tournaments, shattering men's bodies and overthrowing a hundred knights'. The earliest record we have of Owain's experience as a soldier in the field dates from March 1384, when the famous Welsh captain, Sir Gregory Sais, mustered his retainers at Berwick on the Scottish border. Among them were Owain, his brother Tudur, and his poet

Crach Ffinnant. In the following year he again served in the armies of King Richard II in Scotland. These exploits not only gave him military experience but may also perhaps have opened his eyes to the rivalries between the families of Lancaster and Percy and the ambitions of the latter; tensions that were to be of crucial importance later in the course of his rebellion.

The year 1386 saw Owain engaged in a very different kind of activity. This was as a witness in a famous lawsuit between Richard Lord Scrope and Sir Robert Grosvenor, where he mixed freely and easily with some of the highest nobility in the realm. Among those who also gave evidence, interestingly enough, was the great English poet Geoffrey Chaucer. In March 1387 Owain was a prominent member of the retinue of Richard Fitzalan, earl of Arundel, being numbered eighth among the latter's esquires and his brother Tudur twentieth. They both took part under Arundel's command in a naval campaign which achieved the first English success at sea since war had broken out with France in 1369. It proved to be a dangerous adventure but one that was profitable to him not only in financial terms but also in extending his experience of maritime warfare. Later, in November 1387, he may well have been a member of the force which Arundel mustered in the course of his opposition to Richard II. In May of the following year Owain's name headed Arundel's retinue; but the fact that it was crossed through indicates that he did not serve on this occasion. However, he could well have been a member of Richard II's forces in the Irish campaign of 1394. There is no evidence that he was still in service with Arundel in the critical year of 1397 when the earl was arrested and executed at the king's orders. An English chronicler at this time refers to Owain's links with, of all people, Henry of Lancaster, who was later to become King Henry IV (1399–1413), the king of England against whom Owain was to wage long years of war and rebellion. It is possible that Owain was in Henry's service in 1399 just before Lancaster seized the crown.

Throughout these years in the service of leading magnates and the Crown, Owain had gained wide and varied experience of politics and of warfare on land and sea, all of which would have been invaluable to him as the leader of a rebellion. He had also proved himself to be a dashing and courageous soldier in action. Welsh poets, describing his part in the Scottish campaign of 1385, paint a striking picture of him in the heat of the fray. Boldly flaunting on 'his shining helmet a scarlet flamingo feather' with 'his lance broken and snapped off into no more than a dagger', he drove the Scots headlong before him 'howling with fear like wild goats'. So swift and furious were his attacks 'that not a blade of grass or corn would grow in his tracks'. Here, even in his youth, we have a vivid image of him as a fearless leader of men. Already, he was capable of awakening the fervent admiration of his countrymen and of appearing to them as the very soul of Welsh honour and courage. Small wonder that when in 1404 the king of France asked Owain's representatives what kind of present their master would most like from him, he should be told that in nothing did Owain take more pleasure than in the trappings of war. From his youth onwards he had been, above all else perhaps, a soldier.

The same two leading poets, Iolo Goch and Gruffudd Llwyd, who praised his valour on the field of battle were no less attracted by another aspect of his life. This was the more peaceful and civilized side of the Welsh gentleman's existence. Owain had married Margaret Hanmer, daughter of one of the most famous Welshmen of the day and one of Edward III's best-known judges, Sir David Hanmer. The Hanmers were one of the most influential families in north-east Wales. Of English origins, they had lived long enough in Wales to become as Welsh as the Welsh themselves, and members of the family remained close to Owain throughout his rebellion. After her marriage Margaret Hanmer came to live with her husband at Sycharth, where a poet described her as 'the best of wives', 'of a knightly family, honourable, beneficent and noble'. She and Owain brought up a large family of six sons and three daughters, hailed by the same poet as 'a beautiful nest of chieftains'. All six of the boys joined the rebellion and all of them were to die childless.

As Welsh gentry went in those days they were well-to-do. Owain, with a yearly income of £200 from his estates – a sum that has to be multiplied many times, perhaps by as much as two or three hundred, to obtain something like an equivalent amount in modern money – was one of the wealthiest Welsh landowners. Besides, he may also have done well out of the rewards of his military service. He could afford to make his home comfortable and attractive, comparable to a number of similar houses being built in England at this time. It was a timber-framed house, about 30 to 35 feet long and 17½ feet wide, raised on the top of a motte within its surrounding bailey. Iolo

Goch and Gruffudd Llwyd found Sycharth an idyllic haven of ease and hospitality, a 'baron's court, much frequented by bards, the best place in the world'. Iolo described it 'girdled by its moat of shining water' with a bridge and 'lordly gatehouse' leading to a 'fair wooden house on the crest of a green hill upon four wondrous pillars'. This elegant dwelling, 'as high as Westminster cloisters', had a slated roof and – a rare luxury this! – a 'chimney that dispersed smoke'. Within its private chambers were nine wardrobes full of rich clothes and other treasures, 'each like a well-stocked shop in London's Cheapside'. Its most remarkable feature may well have been stained glass windows, compared by Iolo Goch with those of St Patrick's church in Dublin. Nearby, were a church, stables, pigeon-house, deer-park, orchards, fish-pond, rabbit-warren, and heronry; and all around lay 'smiling green meadows and hayfields, and neatly cultivated cornfields'. Its tables were never short of 'good white bread and meat' nor its cellars of wine and the 'first-brewed Shrewsbury beer'. Generous and openhanded, Owain and Margaret welcomed all to their inviting hearth. Sycharth seemed the very embodiment of all those things the Welsh prized most in a gentleman's mansion. Iolo Goch's depiction of it is the most attractive we have of any fourteenth-century Welsh home.

As was to be expected from a Welsh aristocrat of his wealth and lineage, Owain was a pre-eminent patron of the poets who came in considerable numbers to Sycharth, 'meeting-place of bards' as one of their number described it. He showed himself to be deeply absorbed in their ancient lore and tradition; and if the poets appealed to him, he no less surely attracted them. The verses left by two of their outstanding figures, Iolo Goch and Gruffudd Llwyd, reveal that Owain possessed all those attributes that seemed to poets to be the unmistakable hallmarks of impeccable birth, breeding, and leadership. They revelled in his descent from princely forebears in north and south Wales. They applauded those characteristics that announced to the world his truly regal upbringing: his aristocratic hospitality, his generosity to the weak and needy and his ferocity towards the proud and overbearing. They acclaimed his unsurpassed courage on the field of battle and his unsparing demolition of his enemies. Here, surely, in their eyes was the very flower of Cymric gentility.

But these same poets who sang the praises of Sycharth and its owner had other themes of which they reminded him, even during the relatively calm and peaceful days before Wales was plunged into rebellion. They recalled how the forefathers of the Welsh had ruled over a great empire; 'once the strongest and foremost race among men had the British been'. Alas! their descendants had now fallen very low in a world in which jumped-up men of low birth lorded it over men of even princely descent. There may have been much more here than just a coded message signalling the bard's and Owain's increasing frustration during the 1390s at his not being knighted or recognized in any other way. For the old prophecies also held out hopes of deliverance. They foretold the reappearance of a past hero – often known as 'Owain' – who was destined by his valour to lead his people out of bondage and degradation. All that we know of Owain suggests that throughout his life such hopes were always very much in his mind and near to his heart, all the more so perhaps after 1378 when Owain Lawgoch's death had left him as the unchallengeable heir to the prophecies. Who knows what deep-lying chords within his personality may have been struck when Gruffudd Llwyd likened him to Uthr Bendragon or, still more, to Owain ab Urien, both of them early British heroes who had taken vengeance on the Saxons and, by heroic leadership, had reversed earlier disappointments? No matter how widely Owain had moved in the aristocratic world of English upper-class society, he had never outgrown the profound, half-suppressed longings of his own people. Events were soon to bring them dramatically to the surface.

3

The First Waves of Revolt, 1400–1401

The years 1397–1400 were disturbed and crucial ones in the history of England and Wales. Even in the 1380s Richard II had shown himself to be a capricious, headstrong and irresponsible ruler, though the years from 1389 to 1395 had been relatively calm. However, Richard's treaty with France in 1396 had seen the opening of a new and disastrous phase in the history of his reign. In 1397 the king rid himself of his most dangerous opponents in the persons of three of the greatest Marcher lords – Thomas duke of Gloucester, the earl of Arundel, and the earl of Warwick. All three forfeited their estates and the first two their lives. Another two immensely powerful Marcher lords, both with royal blood in their veins, Roger Mortimer, earl of March, and John of Gaunt, duke of Lancaster, died soon after in 1398 and February 1399. As R. R. Davies has observed, 'Never had there been such an earthquake in the map of lordship in Wales'. In the mean time, Richard had launched himself on a career of arbitrary rule which, though not illegal, was in breach of recent custom. He raised bitter opposition to himself by levying heavy taxes, interfering with justice and local government, and installing his favourites in place of the dispossessed magnates. Not even the most influential aristocrats were safe from his displeasure. Among those whom he had banished into exile in 1398 was his own cousin, Henry of Lancaster, John of Gaunt's son. When John died in 1399, Richard refused to allow Henry to return and inherit his estates. In the same year, an Irish chieftain, Art Macmurrough, had seized the opportunity offered by the vacuum caused by the death of the earl of March to rise in rebellion. Richard had no choice but to proceed to Ireland against him with his army.

Richard's absence there gave Henry of Lancaster the opportunity to land in north-east England with an armed force to reclaim his rights, and in his progress through England he met with a good deal of support. Richard returned hurriedly from Ireland to south Wales and made his way northwards to Flint Castle. Here he hoped to establish himself firmly in one of the main centres of his popularity, north Wales and Chester. In fact, he found himself almost completely abandoned, with no choice but to surrender to his enemies. He was taken prisoner and deposed; and Henry of Lancaster became king as Henry IV. The new king claimed his throne by the somewhat dubious title of legitimate descent, vindicated by conquest and acknowledged by some form of popular acclamation in Parliament. The unfortunate Richard, held in close confinement, was dead by the end of January 1400, possibly even as early as the middle of that month. He had perhaps been put to death or even been allowed to starve himself into extinction.

The sudden deposition and subsequent death of the lawful king increased existing turmoil and confusion. In many parts of England a sharp visitation of the plague added to the commotion caused by Richard's downfall and Henry's seizure of power and led to serious outbreaks of violence and disorder. In north Wales, too, Richard had a strong following. Two of the most influential *uchelwyr* in Wales, the brothers Rhys and Gwilym of the famous Tudor family of Penmynydd in Anglesey (from which Henry VII was to be descended), certainly had close ties with him and were in his pay in 1398. Others also may well have been loyal to his memory. When Henry IV, shortly after coming to power, made his son prince of Wales in October 1399 and declared him heir-apparent, a shrewd French knight commented:

> But I think he must conquer [Wales] if he will have it, for in my opinion the Welsh would on no account allow him to be their lord, for the sorrow, evil, and disgrace which the English together with his father had brought on King Richard.

His words, as we shall see, were to be highly prophetic.

But, although it played its part in bringing about rebellion in Wales, the effect of Richard's deposition must not be exaggerated. His measures had by no means been widely popular in Wales, and when he had landed from Ireland and made his way to Flint he had received virtually no support from Wales en route. Little or no attempt was made, either, to prevent his having to surrender to his enemies at Flint, though there exists an old tradition to the effect that Owain was with him at the time of his surrender. This seems distinctly improbable; Owain is hardly likely to have been particularly well disposed towards the king at this time, and his links were more probably with Richard's enemies – Henry of Lancaster and Thomas earl of Arundel.

More important as a cause of Welsh discontent than Richard's downfall may have been Henry IV's unwise attempts to exact heavy communal payments from his Welsh subjects. Commonly levied at the accession of a monarch, they were always strongly resented. A heavy crop of them in 1399–1400, coming on top of earlier exactions by Richard, did nothing to endear the new king. Perhaps the dubious legality of Henry's kingship made these payments all the more disliked. They stirred up still further prevailing feelings of restlessness among the Welsh. Henry was in a weak position at this juncture; not only was his claim to the throne precarious but he was also facing grave difficulties inside and outside his kingdom. He could hardly afford to provoke still further the discontented Welsh *uchelwyr* and their men.

This was nowhere more strikingly borne out than in the relations between Henry, Glyndŵr, and his Marcher neighbour, Lord Grey of Ruthin, in the years 1399–1400. Grey and Owain became involved in a bitter dispute over an area of common land on the borders of their estates. Grey had seized it – unlawfully, Owain contended. To recover possession he placed the matter before Parliament late in the year 1399. When it met in the spring of 1400 it gave the Welshman short shrift and simply refused to listen to his complaint. The Commons were warned against the resentment that so unjust a course of action might awaken among the Welsh by John Trefor, a Welshman

who was bishop of St Asaph. The contemptuous reply
he received was, 'What care we for the barefooted
rascals?' There is, in fact, no trace of the alleged quarrel
in the rolls of Parliament or the central legal records;
but it became evident that the king himself was no
more sympathetic than Parliament. He appeared to
be quite unwilling to take sides against Grey, who was
one of his closest associates. Grey was plainly in a much
stronger position vis-à-vis the king than Thomas, earl
of Arundel, to whom Owain could well have been
looking for support. Welshmen, it seemed, had nothing
to hope for in the way of better treatment from the
new king. Tradition also has it that Owain suffered
another injustice at the hands of Henry and Grey in
the summer of 1400. The king was proposing to go to
war against the Scots and he entrusted to Lord Grey
the summons to Owain to join his army. Grey is said
to have deliberately kept it back, so Owain appeared to
have disobeyed it without offering any explanation;
a course of action which put him in still worse odour
with the king. The story may be true but on the
whole it seems distinctly improbable. Even without
this further grudge, Owain had sufficient cause to
believe he would get justice only if he took the law
into his own hands.

The situation existing in Wales in the late summer
of 1400 was similar to many earlier ones when risings
had been mounted in the days of the former Welsh
princes or even in the fourteenth century. There was
seething discontent against royal authority and Marcher
rule, both of which seemed firmly allied against Welsh
interests. Not only had one tyrannical and unpopular
ruler been overthrown and replaced by another of
doubtful legality but the position had also been made

more unfavourable to the Welsh by the installation of a youthful prince of Wales and the entrusting of the virtual government of north Wales to the highly ambitious Percy family, who had never exercised authority there before. In Principality and March alike the position was insecure and unpromising. In England the king had yet to establish himself, and he was at the same time menaced with war against Scots, Irish and French. It was a classic situ-ation of over-stretched English commitments, which always offered the best prospects for the Welsh successfully to apply pressure.

In the fourteenth century men of aristocratic lineage, wealth and status normally tended to be ambitious and they – and their followers – expected rewards commensurate with what they believed to be their position. If they did not receive them at all, or only to a lesser extent than they thought was their due, they might be driven to join with other discontented men to gain their ends, by political or military pressures or a judicious mixture of both. Such a conjuncture had happened on a number of occasions during Richard II's reign and would occur again during that of Henry IV. Nor had such opposition been unknown in fourteenth-century Wales. There, personal aspir-ations usually merged with and were reinforced by smouldering anti-English resentment. The prophecies which resurfaced again and again over many centuries might have been regularly disappointed and left unfulfilled. But they continued to embody for the Welsh two assumptions which they would never lightly or willingly relinquish. The one was that they were descended from one of the most ancient and hon-ourable stocks in Europe, which gave them a separate identity as a people they wanted to see preserved. The other was that their status as a people made them unwilling to submit to being treated as a conquered race; that whoever their theoretical overlords might be, the only men whose right they recognized to bear direct authority over them were men of their own nationality or those who had identified with it. A similar mingling of private and national resentments may be observed at this time in Ireland and Scotland, both of which came under heavy English pressure, which again and again they tried to shake off. Such reactions are almost universal; in many lands in different ages, men and women have tried to sustain, sublimate and even conceal their narrower personal aspirations by an appeal to higher and more altruistic values.

Owain Glyndŵr would appear to have been faced by just such a crisis in the late 1390s. His earlier years of service to the Crown and some of the great lords, together with his unique standing in Wales, may have led him to expect appropriate patronage and recognition, which had not been forthcoming. Neither Richard II, nor Henry of Lancaster, nor Thomas earl of Arundel had been able, or perhaps even willing, to secure them for him. His disappointment at not having his position acknowledged by being knighted seems evident in the bitter tone of Gruffudd Llwyd's poem to him. To seal his discomfiture and to reveal just how little his interests counted with Henry IV had come the humiliating episode of his quarrel with Lord Grey of Ruthin. This could well have been the last straw; it was at this turning-point that his awareness of Welshness, carefully nurtured by poets and, no doubt, by other followers – clerics, lawyers, soldiers – as well, burst into flames. His anger led him to cast aside all considerations of restraint and earlier loyalties.

It was, without doubt, a difficult decision for him. So much was being put at risk and Owain was in many respects an unlikely rebel. He was over forty years of age, a substantial landowner, comfortably housed and a married man with a large family. Much of his own and his ancestors' background was associated with service to Marcher lords. He had been educated in London, had married an Anglo-Welsh wife and moved in upper-class circles in England. According to Keith Williams-Jones, 'He was a man of conventional habits and conservative tastes, the epitome of conformism and a natural member of the establishment' . Yet, as we have already seen, he had a deep attachment to the culture and traditions of his people which had always been and would always remain at the centre of his loyalties. Moreover, at this time, some of the most influential of his kinsmen, the Tudor brothers of Anglesey, were undoubtedly deeply disaffected and there may have been others like them. Their support and encouragement almost certainly spurred him on and may even first have planted the seeds of rebellion in his mind.

At all events, on 16 September 1400 at Glyndyfrdwy, Owain, his brother, and eldest son met together with a group of friends and relatives. The latter included Hywel Cyffin, dean of St Asaph, Owain's wife's brothers, Gruffudd and Philip Hanmer, and a poet, Crach Ffinnant, who was described, significantly enough, as a 'prophet'. There, they proclaimed Owain prince of Wales, which was, at the very least, a defiant riposte signalling the rejection of Henry IV's earlier creation of his son as prince of Wales. It may also have been a symbolic declaration of the intention to restore the former princedom of Llywelyn the Last. They also prepared plans for an attack on Ruthin, the chief town in Lord Grey's lordship. It was a thriving little market centre which contained a high proportion of Welsh inhabitants and had been the scene of many mixed marriages between Welsh and English. It was full of people who had assembled for the fair to be held on St Matthew's Day (21 September). For his attack on 18 September Owain had under his command some 270 men, many of whom came from the lordship of Denbigh and other surrounding districts. Having damaged and plundered Ruthin, the rebels launched a number of rapid attacks on other nearby boroughs, including Denbigh, Rhuddlan, Flint, Hawarden, Holt, Oswestry, and Welshpool. But on 24 September the rebels were met by an English force under Hugh Burnell and were defeated and scattered. A letter written by Owain in the following year suggests it had been hoped to organize a general rising in Wales at this time. If this was so, the plans were badly concerted, for there was no widespread outbreak in support.

Henry IV had been told the news of the trouble in Wales on his way home from the campaign in Scotland. Remembering earlier warnings from Wales, he took a serious view of the outbreak. He gave orders for the calling up of men from ten English counties for, although Owain and his men were temporarily scattered, a new and dangerous revolt had irrupted in Anglesey. Its ringleaders were the influential Tudor brothers, Rhys and Gwilym. They were Owain's cousins, their mother being a sister to his. They were probably in touch with him and may have intended that their rising should coincide with his. Equally, they may have been acting independently of him, since they were extremely influential in their own right. Having been closely linked with Richard II, they had their own grievances against Henry IV. In the circumstances the king considered the state of north Wales dangerous enough to call for firm action by him. He led the royal army round north Wales to Bangor and Caernarfon, then turned south and completed the circuit by leading it back via Mawddwy to Shrewsbury. He also confiscated the estates of Owain and two or three other leading rebels. But a great many of the Welsh sought the king's pardon and were granted it. The impressive show of force by the royal army appeared to have done its job successfully.

Had the king at this point been able to make a real effort to inquire into Welsh grievances and given some sign of wanting to remedy them, it is possible that the whole revolt might have fizzled out. Whatever the king's views may have been in this respect, he was not a free agent. He depended heavily on getting the support of Parliament because of the dubious legality of his title and even more on account of his need for money. When Parliament met in January and February 1401 it showed itself to be a panicky and vindictive body in all its doings. It is chiefly remembered for the savage laws it passed against religious heretics, and it demanded restrictive action against alien merchants. In its attitude towards Wales it was similarly repressive and narrow-minded. Alarming reports were given of Welsh students leaving the universities to fight for Owain and of Welsh labourers returning from England to join his ranks. Demands were made that the king should agree to laws placing severe restrictions on Welshmen. The king had no choice but to consent. So it was enacted that no Welshman should acquire land or property or hold office in the English boroughs in Wales or in the boroughs of 'Chester, Shrewsbury, Bridgnorth, Ludlow, Leominster, Hereford, Gloucester, Worcester, nor other merchant towns joining to the Marches of Wales'. Any English person in Wales convicted at the suit of any Welsh person was to be tried only by 'English justices or by the judgement of whole Englishmen'. These acts did not go far enough to please the lords of the March, whose help the king would urgently require to put down the Welsh. They pressed him to issue further ordinances which tried to ensure that the castles in Wales and on the border were securely guarded, that the Welsh might not meet together in any number, and that bards and other 'vagabonds' should be re-strained. These measures affected all Welsh people to some degree, but they were intended as an especially severe warning to the *uchelwyr* of the dangers of dis-loyalty. So intense was the alarm felt by the English that, according to the chronicler Adam of Usk, the destruction of the Welsh tongue had been decreed and would have been insisted upon had not God 'mercifully ordained the recall of this decree at the prayer and cry of the oppressed'.

Henry IV had to go along with Parliament and the Marcher lords part of the way at least. Indeed, he himself imposed a further burdensome round of com-munal fines in Wales. But he may have had some hopes of a more conciliatory approach, and the man he chose to carry out his policies in north Wales was Henry Percy, the famous 'Hotspur'. Hotspur's high reputation in war and negotiation made him a good choice for the task. In March an offer of general pardon was made to all except Owain himself and a small number of other major leaders. The common people of the counties of Caernarfon and Merioneth humbly gave thanks and offered to pay the usual taxes. As a result, during this winter Owain may have been reduced to having no more than seven companions. But the appearance of calm was deceptive. In reality, the attitude of Parliament and Marcher lords had been spelt out too clearly for disaffected Welsh *uchelwyr* not to see in it an intolerable threat to them. When spring came round again, bitter guerrilla war broke out. The rioters of the previous autumn had now become open rebels against the Crown.

4

The Rising Tide, 1401–1403

The main threat in the spring of 1401 came at first from the redoubtable Tudor brothers. On Good Friday, 1 April 1401, they captured the important Edwardian castle of Conwy by a ruse when the garrison was at church. The brothers were again operating largely independently of Owain, and their primary aim seems to have been to get better terms for a possible pardon for themselves. Other Welsh forces suffered two sharp defeats: the one at the hands of Hotspur near Cader Idris in May, and the other inflicted on them by John Charlton, lord of Powys, who narrowly missed capturing Owain himself but seized part of his armour. Sorely pressed, Owain switched his operations to south Wales, hitherto untouched by revolt (in the previous October royal permission had been given for the free movement of men there). Following a striking victory at Mynydd Hyddgen in the wilds of the Plynlimmon mountains, Owain attracted to himself widespread backing from the men of Carmarthenshire. So strong did he become that there were wild rumours that he intended to invade England. This was most unlikely; but a letter which he wrote at this time to Henry Dwn, a leading Welsh *uchelwr* of Kidwelly, breathes strongly the confidence he now felt:

> We inform you that we hope to be able, by God's help and yours, to deliver the Welsh people from captivity of our English enemies, who, for a long time now elapsed, have oppressed us and our ancestors. And you may know from your own perception that, now, their time draws to a close and because, according to God's ordinance from the beginning, success turns towards us, no one need doubt a good issue will result, unless it be lost through sloth or strife.

The rebels' success had again given Henry IV cause to be perturbed, and he came down to Worcester to organize an army in June 1401. Not until October, however, was he able to mount an invasion of south Wales. It achieved very little. True, he was able to penetrate deep into west Wales without opposition; but this was because the Welsh guerrilla bands wisely refused to be drawn into pitched battle. He executed one or two prominent followers of Owain, despoiled the famous Welsh Cistercian abbey of Strata Florida, and carried off captives. But he had done almost nothing to reduce Welsh powers of resistance. Later in the year Owain felt strong enough to assault the chief royal fortress in north Wales, Caernarfon Castle. He did not take it but frightened the king's council sufficiently to make them consider the possibility of a negotiated peace. It has even been suggested that some members of the council wanted Hotspur to murder Owain; but he replied hotly that it was not in keeping with his rank to use such evil means against an enemy.

Nothing came of this suggestion of peace. Owain, in the mean time, was obliged to look for new ways of adding to his strength by making allies of some of the king's other enemies. To the king of Scotland he wrote reminding him that they were both descended from the same ancient British kings. The Welsh people, too, had been brought under 'the tyranny and bondage of mine and your mortal foes, the Saxons'. From this tyranny, he added, 'the prophecy saith that I shall be delivered by the aid and succour of your royal majesty'. He ended by asking for the help of Scottish men-at-arms. It was a shrewd and well-directed appeal to a power which had, more than once in the fourteenth century, seriously considered making use of Welsh enmity to the English. A similar plea, stressing again the importance of the prophecies, was sent to the lords of Ireland, including the Irish rebel Art Macmurrough. But the messenger was executed before he could deliver his letters, and no substantial help was received from Scotland or Ireland.

In the year 1402 Owain did well enough without any aid from outside. Early that year the appearance of a brilliant comet was welcomed by the Welsh bards, who hailed it as an excellent omen signifying liberation for the Welsh. Their confidence seemed to be justified when, in April, Owain captured none other than his old enemy Lord Grey of Ruthin, not far from his own town of Ruthin. This was as a result of treachery in his own ranks, according to a Chester chronicler. Owain held Grey to ransom, and Hotspur had hastily to be summoned back to his old post in north Wales to try to hold the English line steady. Owain, ever the opportunist, replied by promptly switching his attack to another quarter, where he met with further striking success. His target this time was the lordship of Maeliennydd (modern Radnor) in the middle March. On 22 June he defeated a large English force at Bryn Glas near the village of Pilleth. Many English leaders were killed, and the most influential lord of the middle March, Edmund Mortimer, was captured and, like Grey, held to ransom. Henry IV, heavily engaged in Scotland and France, could do nothing for the moment to help his hard-pressed lords. Owain, striking while the iron was hot, thrust hard into Gwent and Glamorgan in south-east Wales.

Fearing a still wider collapse, Henry now had to intervene himself. In August 1402 his commissioners of array were mustering three armies for service in Wales. These were somewhat exaggeratedly reputed to have amounted in all to the enormous number of 100,000 men. One assembled at Shrewsbury under the king's command, another at Chester under the prince of Wales, and the third at Hereford commanded by the earl of Stafford. Owain was hopelessly outnumbered, but luckily he was reinforced by an old ally of the Welsh – the weather. The torrential downpours of rain, hail and snow were so indescribably bad that the English armies became convinced that Owain was a magician in league with the powers of darkness! Certainly, the elements fought for him during the disastrous retreat of the cumbersome English armies. Wet, cold, and dispirited, they were bogged down in hostile and unfamiliar country and harassed at every turn by raids and ambushes on the part of the lightly-armed but highly mobile Welsh. The losses suffered in this campaign were reflected in the panic and despair voiced in the English Parliament. A crop of petitions was directed to it, including one which complained of poets and minstrels circulating in Wales and reciting subversive verses to popular gatherings. All that Parliament could do was call for still more stringent measures against the Welsh, which Henry was in no state to refuse. They included precautions against the bards, who were castigated as 'wasters, rhymers, minstrels, and other vagabonds'. They prohibited any 'congregation to be made or suffered to be made by the Welshmen in any place of Wales'. It was further 'ordained and established that from henceforth no Welshman be armed, nor bear defensible armour, to merchant towns, churches, nor congregations . . . except those which be lawful liege people to our sovereign lord the king'. Nor was any Welshman to hold office or have charge of any castles in Wales; while any Englishman who married 'any Welsh woman of the amity of Owain ap (*sic*) Glindour, traitor to our sovereign lord', was to forfeit his rights. A proclamation of 1402 also made it illegal for the English to trade with the Welsh; but this was often disregarded and large quantities of goods were smuggled from England into Wales. Parliament pressed in addition that the ransom money demanded for Lord Grey's release should be paid. Of the huge sum of 10,000 marks (one mark would have been worth about 66p), 6,000 were paid at once and it was agreed that the balance should be paid later.

In contrast with his eagerness to obtain Grey's release, Henry's reluctance to ransom Owain's other notable prisoner, Mortimer, was painfully marked. But Mortimer was potentially a great threat to the king, because his youthful nephew, also Edmund, the young earl of March, as a descendant of Lionel, second son of Edward III, probably had a better claim to the throne than Henry himself as the son of John of Gaunt, third son of Edward. Indeed, back in Richard II's reign the Mortimer earl of March had been mooted by some as a preferable alternative to the unpopular Richard. Seeing Mortimer held captive by the Welsh, therefore, may have been more of a relief than a worry to Henry. Mortimer himself, despairing of ever otherwise being freed, now entered into an alliance with Owain and sealed it by marrying the Welsh leader's daughter. If rumours that Richard II was alive proved to be untrue, he would seek to place his nephew, the earl of March, on the throne and would secure to Owain 'his right in Wales'. He announced this change of front to his associates and tenants and urged them to accept it. Many of them were Welsh and may gladly have done so. Through Mortimer, Owain was able to establish secret negotiations with a still more powerful figure, Henry Hotspur, who was married to Mortimer's sister. In the mean time, the prince of Wales, the future Henry V, having just been appointed the king's lieutenant in Wales in March 1403, had shown his mettle with a sharp raid into Wales. In the course of it he burnt Owain's residences at Sycharth and Glyndyfrdwy. He urged the king to give him the men for a final decisive attack on the Welsh rebels, but his father was too preoccupied with his Scottish campaigns to respond. The delay could be dangerous because it was at this point that Hotspur came out into the open against Henry IV.

This month of July 1403 presented Henry with a desperately serious crisis. In the north he was faced with heavy pressure from the Scots. But his leading northern vassals, on whom he chiefly relied to keep the Scots at bay, were in open opposition to him.

Since the autumn of 1402 the Percy family had had a number of grievances against Henry. It was being suggested that among them were their opposition to his Welsh policies and their wish to reach an understanding with Glyndŵr. They particularly resented the king's refusal to let them ransom Edmund Mortimer on the grounds that the latter had committed treason. One chronicler went so far as to suggest that the Percies themselves had ambitions on the crown. Once successful, they would get rid of the Mortimers and crown Hotspur, or his son, as king by virtue of the hereditary right of Hotspur's wife. In the mean time, Hotspur issued a proclamation referring to the king as Henry of Lancaster and spreading the story that Richard II was alive. Simultaneously, he was collecting an army to unite with Owain and Mortimer and the archers and men-at-arms of Wales and Cheshire.

From Henry's point of view the situation was extremely hazardous, and letters from his harassed officials in Wales show how panic-stricken they were. If Hotspur were to link with Owain and Mortimer, the king would be heavily outnumbered and all might be lost. Spurred on by the gravity of his peril, Henry acted with astonishing speed. He intercepted Hotspur at Shrewsbury and forced him to do battle before Percy senior, the earl of Northumberland, or the Welsh contingents could join him. Hotspur was decisively beaten and killed in the action. His defeat was obviously a great gain for Henry IV. How serious a setback was it for Owain? It can, of course, be argued that a glorious opportunity to inflict a crushing defeat on Henry had been missed. Yet even if it had been seized it is doubtful whether the allies in an unstable feudal alliance of this kind would have held together for very long, particularly in view of the reported ambitions of the Percies. As for Wales itself, the battle of Shrewsbury made little or no difference to Owain's strength there. By September 1403 the king was obliged to assemble at Worcester yet another large force for the attempted reconquest of south Wales. True to form, it marched unopposed up the valley of the Usk and on to Carmarthen. Orders were given for carpenters and masons to put royal castles in a state of good repair. Supplies of wheat, oats, wine, and fish for the garrisons were brought in from Bristol and south Wales. The lands of some of the rebels were seized and transferred to Welshmen loyal to the king, while other rebels were pardoned. The withdrawal of royal troops, however, once again took place quickly. As soon as they had gone, the rebels were as much in command as ever. Only the well-fortified castles could hold out against them.

Some of the castles themselves, even, were in serious danger. The castles of Llansteffan, Dryslwyn, Newcastle Emlyn, and Carreg Cennen actually fell to Owain's men in 1403 as a result of the presence of Welsh sympathizers among their garrisons. Nearly all these castles were situated inland. But the most powerful ones were placed on or near the coast and could be kept supplied by sea. One of the rebels' greatest weaknesses had been lack of sea-power to cut off these supplies. Even this was now partly made good, when free-booters from Brittany who had been attacking Bristol and other English ports joined forces with Henry Dwn at Kidwelly. Another French squadron, under Jean d'Espagne, was helping the men of north Wales. Between them, they were applying heavy pressure on the great strongholds of Harlech, Caernarfon and Beaumaris, bringing up ordnance for the purpose. So acute was the pressure that, on 12 January 1404, one of the keepers of Conwy Castle had written in alarm that the whole of Caernarfonshire intended to raid Anglesey and sweep the place bare 'lest Englishmen should be refreshed therewith'. At the opposite end of Wales, in a surprise attack on Cardiff, the town was burnt and the castle forced to surrender. Winter was now setting in – usually the worst time of the year for rebel guerrillas. But by the turn of the year 1403 Owain's mid-winter strength had never been sturdier. He could look forward to still greater successes when the spring campaigning season came round again.

Plate 1
The memorial to Llewelyn the Last at Cefn-bedd, Builth Wells.

Plate 2
The Great Seal of Owain Glyndŵr.

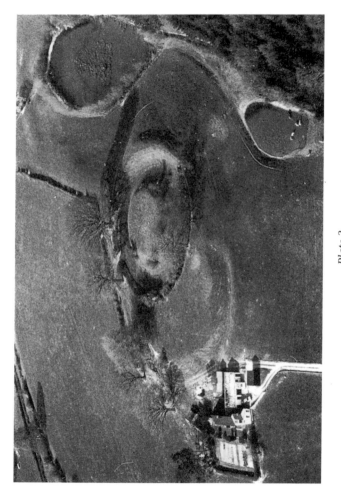

Plate 3
Sycharth, Owain Glyndŵr's birthplace.

Plate 4
Caernarfon Castle.

Plate 5
Harlech Castle.

Plate 6
Owain Glyndŵr's Parliament House, Machynlleth.

Plate 7

A performance of Henry IV, Part I at the Royal Shakespeare Theatre in 1975. From left to right: Glyndŵr, Mortimer, Worcester, Hotspur.

Plate 8
Map of Wales at the time of Glyndŵr's Revolt, 1400–15.

5

High-water Mark, 1404–1406

If the year 1404 promised well for Owain, its prospects for Henry looked bleak enough. Threatened on
all sides by his enemies, he also found himself the
target of severe criticism from the Parliament which
met in January. In response to his requests for money
he met with a barrage of attacks on his own extrava-
gance and financial mismanagement. Parliament
was hardly fair to Henry. The two reasons which
chiefly accounted for the desperate state of his finances went deeper than personal incompetence.
The one was the serious drop in customs revenues as
a result of the operations of French pirates. The other
and more important reason was the drain of money
caused by constant war and rebellion.

News from Wales in the spring did nothing to lighten
the gloom. The great castles of north Wales were still
tightly besieged. Some idea of Caernarfon's plight may
be gleaned from letters written by its defenders at
this time. They had to use a woman to bring news by
word of mouth,

for neither man nor woman dare carry letters on account of the rebels of Wales . . . and in the town and castle there are not in all more than 28 fighting men, which is too small a force . . . so that the said castle and town are in imminent danger.

Harlech and Aberystwyth were even nearer collapse. In April they were still clinging on desperately while the royal council was anxiously trying to get ships from Bristol to relieve them and to counter the efforts of David Perrot, a Pembrokeshire gentleman of English stock with naval experience, who had perhaps defected with Thomas Percy and was now preparing ships for sea in the rebel cause. The English relief measures were of little avail and later this spring, or early summer, both castles fell. Harlech seems to have held out longer than Aberystwyth and was the later of the two to succumb. Their capture was of enormous value to Owain. It raised his own men's morale and depressed English spirits. It gave him two powerful bases and enabled him to maintain his family and his princely court in safety. He was now able to rule Wales from Caernarfon to Cardigan virtually unchallenged. So secure was he that he could confidently call representatives to a Parliament at Machynlleth. As Adam of Usk rather unsympathetically said: 'Owain and his hill-men . . . usurping the right of conquest and other marks of royalty . . . held or counterfeited or made pretence of holding parliaments.'

His success encouraged him to embark on a broader, more constructive, and more imaginative line of policy. He was now far more than an aggrieved *uchelwr* claiming personal rights, or a member of a group of discontented feudal nobles bringing pressure to bear on the king. He was clearly setting himself up as the prince of an independent state with an ambitious national programme. In pursuing this end he could have been recalling the policies of the earlier princes of Gwynedd. Scotland, too, provided him with a model of broadly the kind of position he wished to enjoy. Or he may well have had in mind the way in which some French principalities were then trying to set themselves up in independence of the king of France. In formulating and carrying out these plans he was greatly helped by a group of able clerics who now came over to his side. They included Gruffudd Young, who became his chancellor, John Trefor, bishop of St Asaph, and Lewis Byford, bishop of Bangor. Men like these were highly trained and experienced administrators and civil servants. They may have suggested some of these schemes to Owain, though there is no reason to suppose that he was in any way incapable of devising them for himself. But whether the clerics did or did not originate the plans, they were certainly extremely useful in carrying them out.

If this programme for a national state was to be fulfilled, Owain would have to do more than fight guerrilla operations. To maintain his independence against England he would have to have sufficient force to beat off invasion by English armies. He could hardly hope to do so without the help of a powerful and reliable ally, and the obvious choice for such an ally was France. What would be chiefly needed from her was added sea-power, experienced men-at-arms to make up for Welsh deficiencies in numbers, and engines-of-war to reduce powerful castles. France, on her side, stood to gain much in return. She could hope to do with Wales what she had long done through the 'auld alliance' with Scotland against England, thus forcing her enemy to fight on three fronts. Such a course of action had commended itself to her more than once in the fourteenth century, and she had already seen the possibility of helping herself by helping Owain. In 1401 the king of France had sent a Welsh knight, Dafydd ab Ifan Goch, to the king of Scotland on behalf of Owain, and again, in 1403–4, Jean d'Espagne's squadron had worked with the Welsh rebels. The latter's growing strength inspired French hopes that a closer agreement with Wales would give the king of France the same sort of base in the English king's domains as he had for attacking France in Calais and Gascony.

In these circumstances it is not surprising that an alliance was quickly concluded. Owain sent his brother-in-law, John Hanmer, and his chancellor, Gruffudd Young, as his representatives to France. In a letter to the French king, Charles VI, Owain styled himself prince of Wales, by the grace of God. His coat of arms as prince, significantly, was the old royal arms of Gwynedd, the four lions rampant, and not the single lion of Powys. The negotiations took place in June–July 1404, and a treaty was concluded on 14 July. It bound both sides in a 'sure, good and most powerful union against Henry of Lancaster, adversary and enemy of both parties'. Each agreed not to make peace independently of the other. No actual mention was made of military aid, but this could be expected to follow automatically.

Back in Wales, although a number of castles in north and south were holding out grimly, pressure on the English border counties was steadily mounting.

In June had come a pathetic letter from the sheriff and gentlemen of the county of Hereford to the king. It told how the Welsh had entered the country burning houses and taking prisoners, with the threat of worse to follow. The men of Shropshire were equally hard pressed. They had to agree to a three months' truce not, notice, with the rebels but with the 'land' of Wales. It looked as if Owain was bent on taking the war into England, or at least on terrorizing the English border into recognizing his independence. He had reached the peak of his power, and the summer was always his best campaigning season. If a French force landed now, there was no telling how damaging a thrust he might make into England. It looked like an ideal opportunity for French intervention, and a strong French force of sixty ships actually left harbour. But it concerned itself too much with paying off old scores against English sailors and it wasted its energies in cruising the Channel. Three landings by French and Bretons that were made on the south coast of England were easily repelled. If the effort had been concentrated in support of Owain it might well have paid much more handsome dividends. A unique opportunity had been lost. Nevertheless, in Wales itself Owain more than held his own for the rest of 1404.

The year 1405 was one of mixed fortunes for the rebels. It opened with a plot which was probably closely connected with the Welsh leader's plans. The countess of Gloucester made a daring bid to bring the two young sons of the Mortimer earl of March to Glamorgan, where Owain's power had recently been felt in the capture of Cardiff. The boys' uncle, Edmund Mortimer, was in close alliance with Owain and the elder of the boys, as we have seen, had a strong legal claim to the English throne. He was undoubtedly needed as a pawn in another scheme now being hatched. This was the three-sided alliance between Owain, Mortimer, and the earl of Northumberland, in which the last-named took the initiative. Sworn to and sealed on 28 February 1405, it was known as the Tri-partite Indenture and it proposed to divide the realm into three parts between the allies. Its terms suggest that it was basically an understanding between Northumberland and Owain. The former was to receive the north of England along with much of the north Midlands. Though Mortimer was to get southern England and his nephew to be made king, significantly enough no mention was made of including in his share the great Marcher properties of the family. Owain's proposed share was remarkably interesting. It would include not only Wales but also a large part of England

> namely from the Severn Sea, as the river Severn leads from the sea, going to the north gate of the city of Worcester, and from that gate to the Ash Tree . . . which grows on the high way leading from Bridgnorth to Kynvar; thence by the high way which is commonly called the old or ancient road, direct to the head or source of the Trent; thence to the head or source of the river commonly called Mersey, thence as that river leads to the sea.

At first sight this may seem a strange allocation for the ruler of a Welsh national state, but there were good reasons for it. First, Owain was anxious to fulfil some of the old prophecies concerning the recovery of their ancient lands by the Welsh. There were also at least three important practical considerations. One was that many Welshmen had been settling in these border areas before the Rebellion, and their English inhabitants had petitioned Parliament to keep the intruders out. Another was that the main assembly points for armies used against Wales, like Worcester, Shrewsbury or Hereford, were situated in this region. Finally, this agreement was virtually one between Owain and Northumberland, and in dealing with so sharp and unreliable an ally Owain needed a strong and defensible territorial power to match that of the northern magnate.

In fact, this agreement was never more than a pipe-dream. None of the parties to it achieved much success in the months that followed. Owain himself suffered two severe setbacks in south-east Wales. The first took place near Grosmont in March, when Prince Henry described how he had sent three of his leading lieutenants against the Welsh and killed 'of them by fair account in the field . . . some say eight hundred, others a thousand'. The second was a heavier and more serious defeat in May at Pwll Melyn near Usk at the hands of a strong English force under Lord Grey of Codnor. Here, Owain's son, Gruffudd, was captured and subsequently imprisoned, and his brother, Tudur, was killed. In this same month the king was raising yet another army for service in Wales. Owain was saved from it only by a rising of the men of northern England under Archbishop Scrope of York. This northern rising was utterly crushed. Its failure did nothing to brighten the prospects of the Tri-partite Indenture, which had never anyway had much chance of lasting success.

It was not on Northumberland, however, that Owain pinned his brightest hopes; it was to France he looked for decisive help. In that quarter the situation looked favourable, since agreement had been reached between the dukes of Orleans and Burgundy, whose selfish dissensions had for long crippled French policy. With French aid Owain hoped to be able to force England to agree to a lasting peace. To make his own forces as strong as possible in readiness for his French allies, he called a Welsh Parliament to meet at Harlech about 1 August. To it he summoned four leading men from every commote or administrative district under his control. He explained to them his plan for forcing England to agree to make peace in face of the combined power of French and Welsh forces. He must also have persuaded them to agree to provide him with as much money and as many men as possible for the coming campaign. In this he seems to have been reasonably successful, for he was reported as having 10,000 men under his command to meet the French. The latter left Brest on 22 July with 140 ships carrying 800 men-at-arms, 600 crossbowmen, and 1,200 lightly-armed troops, and reached Milford Haven early in August. The joint forces, having quickly taken the town of Haverfordwest and the town and castle of Carmarthen, pressed eastwards. They crossed the English border and advanced to Woodbury Hill within eight miles of Worcester. It looked as if the hour of decision had arrived. Owain had never before entered England with so great a force; indeed, not since the Norman Conquest had a foreign army penetrated so deeply into the heart of English territory. Yet no decisive encounter took place. Owain seems to have concluded he was too far from his base and still not strong enough in numbers to risk a pitched battle. Perhaps he had never intended

to fight one. He may confidently have hoped that
the very existence of the Franco-Welsh force on
English soil would have been enough to make Henry
IV sue for peace. If so, he had seriously miscalculated.

He now withdrew to the safety of Wales, while in his
rear Henry assembled a very large army in September
1405. But if Owain's weakness had been shown up
in England, Henry's was once more revealed in Wales.
The weather again fought for the Welsh, and the
English army had to beat a hasty and confused retreat.
As it withdrew, Owain's men laid eager hands on its
baggage train, containing provisions, jewels, and other
valuables. Food and armour, even, were said to have
been brought to the Welsh by men from Gloucestershire
and Herefordshire. Those supplies were going to be
needed by the rebels to see them through the winter
and to buoy up their spirits, for in November a large
body of French knights returned to France. They left
behind a solid corps of infantry which made a sufficiently great impression on the English inhabitants of south Pembrokeshire for them to offer Owain
£200 in silver for a truce to last until May 1406. But,
early in 1406, the rest of the French went home, and
only feeble attempts were afterwards made to provide
replacements for them. The events of 1405 had been
a moment of truth for Welsh and French alike. The
French had seen that Owain could not bulldoze the
way into England for them. He had realized that
they could not force a lasting truce for him. After this,
there were to be no more combined military operations
to speak of.

In 1406, however, the end of the alliance between
France and Wales was not yet in sight. In March they
were engaged in negotiations over Church matters of

considerable interest and importance. Since 1378 the
Church had had two rival popes, the one at Rome
and the other at Avignon. European powers made
their choice between them on political grounds, so
England supported the former, whereas her rivals,
France and Scotland, backed the latter. Charles VI of
France now persuaded Owain to consider the possibility of transferring his allegiance to Pope Benedict
XIII at Avignon. On 8 March 1406 he sent a letter by
two Welsh envoys, Hugh or Hywel 'Eddoyer', a
Dominican friar, and Maurice Kerry, to the Welsh.
Leading magnates and clerics met at Pennal, near
Machynlleth, to consider the suggestion. On 31 March
they put forward some highly interesting terms for
supporting Benedict. The most important of these
was that he should create an ecclesiastical province
in Wales independent of Canterbury. At its head 'the
Church of St David's shall be restored to its original
dignity, which from the time of St David . . . was a
metropolitan church . . . As a metropolitan church it
had and ought to have the undermentioned
suffragan churches, namely Exeter, Bath, Hereford,
Worcester, . . . Coventry and Lichfield, St Asaph,
Bangor, and Llandaff'. The pope was further asked
to agree to provide in Wales only such 'prelates,
dignitaries, and beneficed clergy and curates who
know our language'. He was also asked to allow 'two
universities or places of general study, namely one
in north Wales and the other in south Wales, in
cities, towns or places herafter to be decided'. This
'Pennal policy', as it is usually called, reflects the ideas
of Owain's leading clerical advisers, especially his
chancellor, Gruffudd Young. It was a bold and imaginative plan which, if it had succeeded, would have

freed the Church in Wales from the control of the English state. This would have made it possible for an independent Welsh ruler to recruit and reward the highly-trained clerics whom he would have to have to act as his top-level administrators and civil servants. These men would have been trained in Welsh universities independently of the two great English universities. In envisaging these new institutions, Owain and his advisers may have known of universities like those at Heidelberg and Leipzig then being founded by princes. In Scotland, too, there were many who shared the Welsh desire for an autonomous archbishop and an independent university, and when the University of St Andrews was founded in 1413, it owed much to the good offices of Pope Benedict XIII. Had Glyndŵr's plan succeeded, Wales would have had universities older and earlier than those of many European countries, including the famous Scottish ones.

These ambitious schemes came to nothing. They were being put forward at a time when Owain's successful progress had come to a standstill. All around, the skies were beginning to darken for his cause. He himself was defeated in battle in April, and two months later, his ally, the earl of Northumberland, was also defeated in Wales by a force of Cheshire and Shropshire men led by Charlton, lord of Powys. No significant help was provided, either, by the French. The other thorn in Henry IV's flesh, the Scots, saw their own hopes sadly dwindling when the young heir to the Scottish throne fell into English hands. Soon after, his father died, and the new king of Scotland was to remain a prisoner in England for eighteen years. A Welsh annalist had already shrewdly commented that the tide had turned for the rebel leader. Before the end of the year 1406 there were signs of Welsh confidence being drastically sapped and English morale sharply rising. Owain, on his side, lost control of a great part of his outlying territories. Gower, the Tywi Valley, and large parts of Cardiganshire gave in, depriving him of the greater part of his authority in the south. In Anglesey there was a large-scale submission to the king. It was not military defeat which caused this surrender but loss of heart for the struggle, coupled perhaps with a shortage of food. The severe restrictions imposed by the English on the export of provisions from England, and especially of arms, were now taking their toll. The English Parliament, on its side, made strong demands that the prince of Wales be given greater authority in Wales to crush the rebellion once and for all. Both Parliament and the prince seemed to sense the possibility that final victory was within reach.

6

Between Two Tides, 1406–1407

Before we go on to consider the details of Owain's decline, however, we might pause for a moment to assess what he had achieved and why. First, where and how did he draw his support? Linked as he was to the princely families of both north and south, he could appeal to all parts of the country. His lineage made him better fitted than anyone else in Wales to fill the role of the liberator promised in ancient prophecy. This notion, so ardently cherished by him and his contemporaries, figures prominently at many crucial points in his rebellion. It had given hope to many disgruntled men and women among all classes willing to see in alien rule the cause of all their grievances. By 1403 virtually all of Wales, except for a minority, had joined his cause. But it was, nevertheless, to the *uchelwyr* that he looked chiefly; without their lead the rest of the population would have been discontented but inert. And it was from the *uchelwyr* that he drew his toughest and most steadfast supporters: men like his Tudor cousins or his Hanmer brothers-in-law in north Wales, or Rhys

Gethin or Henry Dwn of Kidwelly in the south. Their lead was obviously popular and widely supported by lesser men of all ranks.

In addition to the laity, the clergy had lent valuable support. Some of the higher clergy, themselves men of gentle birth, had been solidly behind Owain. The dean of St Asaph was with him on the very first outbreak, while it was in the house of the archdeacon of Bangor, David Daron, that the Tri-partite Indenture was signed. Owain had shown particular concern to recruit those promising young Welsh scholars at Oxford who, greatly excited by the Rebellion, were said to have met at the house of Alice Walsh at Oxford, and there 'with many wicked meetings and counsels to have plotted against our Lord the King and the Realm for the destruction of the kingdom and the English language'. From the 'merest boys of Wales' to senior figures like the curiously-named Dafydd 'Llygaid Brith' ('Speckled eyes'), they had rallied to Owain's cause. Others who had been warm in Owain's support were Franciscan friars, who were devoted to Richard II's memory. A number of the abbots of Cistercian monasteries, too, – Strata Florida, Aberconwy, Caerleon – some of the largest and most Welsh in sympathy of the religious houses of Wales, had lent themselves to his cause. Among those clerics who came over to him in 1404, like Gruffudd Young or John Trefor, he counted some of his shrewdest advisers. Priests of humbler station in numberless country parishes joined with their flock in upholding his fight. For example, among those who surrendered in Anglesey in 1406 were listed a large number of clerics from the highest cathedral clergy down to parish priests.

But enthusiasm for Owain or dislike for Henry IV and the English was one thing; translating it into successful military resistance was quite another matter. Owain had for many years been faced with the task of raising and maintaining troops. Just how tremendously expensive this could be we can gauge to some extent from the surviving accounts of the royal armies. Thus, for instance, it cost £6,825 to maintain the prince of Wales's force of 2,400 archers and men-at-arms in Wales for six months in 1407–8. Owain's men were almost certainly nothing like as expensive per head as this. Yet on a number of occasions he was able to raise as many as 8,000 or 10,000 troops, and he was even reputed by Adam of Usk to have had as many as 30,000 at one time. The men in such an army, however mobile and lightly-armed they may have been, had nevertheless to be armed and fed, and would also have expected pay or reward. To this aspect of Owain's achievements historians have paid curiously little attention; perhaps because we can only guess at the answer to the question, how had it been done?

First, and possibly foremost, Owain depended on the pillage and plunder of towns and lordships in Wales and the English border that were hostile to him. Adam of Usk describes him as being 'like a second Assyrian' harrying town and countryside with 'fire and sword . . . carrying off the spoil of the land and especially the cattle to the mountains of Snowdon'. There was nothing new or shocking about this by the standards of fifteenth-century warfare. As A. G. Bradley has noted, 'War was a trade, ravage its hand-maid, and human life of but small account'. He had also managed to plunder the baggage-train of English forces very successfully on more than one occasion.

He had captured valuable prisoners like Lord Grey and held them to ransom. He had on occasions held whole districts to ransom, as it were, by concluding local truces guaranteeing to leave various regions in peace on condition that he was paid large sums of money. In this way he put pressure on the traditional enemies of the Welsh – the inhabitants of south Pembrokeshire, who offered him £200 in silver for a truce lasting six months. No doubt, he used this and other ransom money to equip and reward his own men.

Yet it is difficult not to believe that a leader so astute and far-seeing would have wanted to ensure other more permanent and reliable sources of income. These he would have to have not merely to keep his troops in the field but also to meet the other expenses of running an independent state. According to Adam of Usk, Wales was worth £60,000 a year to England before the Rebellion. When the Rebellion was at its height virtually none of this could be collected by the English government. What we should dearly like to know more about is whether, and in what way, Owain managed to divert any part of it into his own coffers. It would have been surprising if he had not that object in view in summoning his Parliaments – after all, that was the main object for which English Parliaments were always called. It is quite certain that the ecclesiastical policy he outlined at Pennal was partly intended to stop revenue from going to England and to divert it to him instead. He would, of course, have to be careful not to alienate his own followers by demanding heavy taxes from them. It may be that part of the price for the support he got was an agreement that moneys they had previously paid to the

English Crown were now to be kept by the Welsh tax-payers and tenants themselves. An English officer in Wales, Reynald of Bayldon, one of the keepers of Conwy Castle, gives some hint of this when he suggests keeping an English force in rebel-held areas 'to make a levy of my lord's debts, and for to take their wages of the same debt, rather than to let the rebel have all'. It was even rumoured that England itself harboured secret supporters of Owain who sent him large sums of money to keep his uprising going, and men were actually brought before English courts for such an offence. But it seems to us now to be un-likely that any significant support of this kind was forthcoming.

These financial obstacles taken into account, it becomes all the more remarkable that Owain kept his rebellion going as long as he did. There were many other popular rebellions in other parts of Europe during the fourteenth century and there had been earlier risings in Wales, yet hardly any of them lasted for more than a few months. It was only in the rarest and most exceptional cases that a popular rising had not expended its force within a matter of weeks. That Owain's continued for so many years is proof of the strength of discontent and of patriotic feeling among the Welsh. It is an even greater tribute to the qualities of Owain's leadership. Obviously he was a man of indomitable courage and determination. No less clearly he was a military commander of consider-able ability. He lost some battles, of course, but he fought his campaigns with great skill and daring. He relied mostly on guerrilla tactics, lightning raids, and rapid switches of direction. He avoided pitched battles in which he was likely to be at a disadvantage in weapons, armour and numbers, and he made skilful use of the terrain and climate of Wales. All the same, he was not limited to the narrow vision of a successful military captain; he had the qualities of a statesman, too. His political programme of 1404–6 was broad and imaginative, and it seems not only to have convinced his own countrymen but the French and Scots as well. That it should ultimately have failed is no discredit to him or his men. What is surprising is not his downfall but that he was successful for so long.

This stands out all the more clearly when we consider the power of the forces working against him in Wales. We have first of all to remember the bitter cost of the struggle to those who were his sympathizers. If he plundered and pillaged to keep his rebellion going, the royal forces retaliated still more ferociously to stamp it out. Rebellion in this age was regarded as unpardonable by rulers and any degree of force or fraud might be employed to suppress it. An English official in Wales, one John Fairford, called on the king to 'ordain a final destruction of all the false (Welsh) nation'. Henry and his son needed little urging. Adam of Usk describes how in 1402, with Owain and his 'poor wretches keeping close [i.e., hidden] in their caves and woods, the king laid waste the land and returned victoriously with a countless spoil of cattle'. The prince of Wales told with undisguised pride and delight how he proceeded to the vale of Edeirnion in Merioneth and 'there laid waste a fine and populous country'. Many other similar instances could be cited. Such devastation weighed heavily on a peasantry who had known half a century or more of great hardships. Some of them had joined the rebels only because they were forced to, or from fear for their goods and property. In that letter from Reynald of Bayldon already quoted he wrote:

> Also I have heard myself that many of the gentlemen and commons of Merioneth and Caernarfonshire swear that all the men of the foresaid shires, except four or five gentlemen and a few vagabonds, would fain come to peace so that Englishmen were left in the country to help to keep them from misdoers.

Many others, besides, understandably weakened under pressure. Either they sought the king's pardon or else they wavered uneasily. The men of the hill district of Brecon lordship, for instance, agreed in February 1404 to submit to the king if he could defeat the rebels in the area but otherwise to remain faithful to Owain. Others successfully trimmed their sails and tacked over to the royal side when the wind blew against the rebels. A notable example was William Gruffudd, a member of the Tudor family who first supported Owain but went over to the king in 1406. It was a smart move on his part and it founded the fortunes of the Gruffudd family of Penrhyn Castle, the core of whose home is still part of that huge castle today. There was a great deal of changing of sides of this kind by rebels great and small.

There were, however, a minority in Wales who had been hostile from the outset and who never took the insurgents' side. Most national rebellions have within them an element of civil war of this kind. Among Owain's most determined enemies were the burgesses of the boroughs of Wales, whether they were English by birth, as was usually the case, or Welsh. An outstanding example among them, Thomas Dyer of Carmarthen, was said to have lost as much as £1,000 as a result of the Rebellion. Others opposed to Owain were English families settled in Wales, often in close connection with the Marcher lords. Yet some of his opponents were prominent Welshmen. His own cousin, Hywel Selau of Nannau, was traditionally believed to have tried to kill him. Instead, he was himself killed by Owain and his corpse put in that hollow oak-tree commemorated in Sir Walter Scott's poem, *Marmion*:

> All nations have their omens drear,
> Their legends wild of love or fear;
> To Cambria look – the peasant see
> Bethink him of Glyndowerdy,
> And shun the spirit's Blasted Tree.

Another leading Welshman, this time from south-east Wales, who was bitterly opposed to Owain, was Dafydd Gam. He was the ancestor of the famous Herbert family and was later killed fighting at Agincourt (1415) for Henry V's army. Some families were divided amongst themselves, so that while Robert ap Maredudd ab Ieuan supported Owain, his brother Ifan ap Maredudd, was a staunch royalist who had his houses burned by the insurgents and was killed defending Caernarfon Castle against their attacks.

The Rebellion posed a genuine conflict of loyalties for some leading Welsh families. They had for three or four generations been loyal to the king of England or a great Marcher family. Owain Glyndŵr had no legal right to their allegiance of a kind exercised over his subjects by, say, the king of Scotland. He had only a moral claim on their loyalty. There was always an added danger, therefore, that in adversity they might succumb to English offers of pardon or reconciliation.

This was a temptation right from the beginning; but it became all the more difficult to resist once the high point of the Rebellion was passed in 1406. All the more so because Henry IV's position was much stronger from now onwards. Hereafter, he could much more confidently offer pardon with one hand and crush resistance with the other.

7

The Tide Turns and Ebbs, 1407–1415

Owain's earlier success had owed much to Henry IV's weakness and ineptitude. Inside his kingdom, Henry's seizure of power by force had created its own problems. It left Richard II's supporters hostile and violent, and it also encouraged some of the magnates who had at first supported Richard's deposition later to contemplate the possibility of dispossessing Henry in the same way. External enemies in France, Scotland and Ireland, eager to seize on English weakness, could all find it convenient not to recognize Henry as a lawful king. Confronted by this sea of troubles Henry found his finances shaky and insufficient. Before 1406 he had never been able to give undivided attention and resources to Wales for very long. He had tended to alternate uncertainly between policies of repression and reconciliation, with the former much more apparent than the latter and neither having been carried out very consistently or thoroughly. His campaigns against Wales had been indecisive; little more than sorties in force to relieve his beleaguered garrisons. After 1405 his fortunes greatly improved.

External dangers became far less acute when he had the king of Scotland safely within his grasp in captivity and France became increasingly torn by savage internal rivalries between Armagnacs and Burgundians. Opposition in England, which had earlier created an atmosphere of suspicion and treachery, though not yet ended, was nothing like so serious a threat as it had been, and some of the worst enemies like the Percies had been completely overthrown. Fewer expensive military commitments, at home and abroad, meant a distinct improvement in the royal finances which, from 1405 onwards, were much healthier and better organized. The financial crisis of 1403–4 had led to the formation of a war fund or secret treasury. Much larger payments, more regular and better sustained, were made from the Exchequer, which contributed £72,000 to the war in Wales between 1401 and 1413, most of it after 1405. Henry's growing security boded ill for the hopes of the Welsh insurgents.

It was in Wales, too, that his heir, Prince Henry, learned most about the trade of warfare. It proved to be his training-ground, not only as a soldier but also as a business-man and a financial organizer of war. More and more he was revealing those powers of command which were to make him one of the outstanding generals of the age. The royal forces had always enjoyed certain advantages over the Welsh which now told increasingly in their favour. Even the geography of Wales, whose upland terrain had helped the Welsh so greatly in their guerrilla tactics of quick thrusts, sudden raids and the avoidance of pitched battles, was now tending to work against them. The lines of communication ran east and west and not north and south. Wales was more easily linked to

England, therefore, than united within itself; a factor which counted heavily in the war of attrition now increasingly being waged against the rebels. There were also three other factors of decisive importance: sea-power, castles, and superiority in numbers and arms. Owain had always been short of sea-power because the men best able to provide ships – the seaport merchants – were among those bitterly opposed to him. He had consequently had to look for help from the French fleets, which was no longer forthcoming. Without control of the sea it had proved impossible to prevent some of the most powerful English bases in Wales from holding out. Supplied by sea, they could fight on far in the rear of Welsh armies with a surprisingly small garrison of defenders. Caernarfon Castle was held against the rebels by a force reduced at one time to only twenty-eight men, and Harlech by as few as sixteen. The other threat to these castles was the use of engines-of-war for scaling, battering down, or blowing up their defences. Deficient in these, too, Owain had counted on getting help from the French. But when in turn it came to his own castles being attacked, he found the English armies being equipped with superior means of destruction. Cannon were being used against his strongholds of Harlech and Aberystwyth, as payments made for the services of English 'cannoniers' show. In his life of Owain Glyndŵr, A. G. Bradley noted that 'Great guns were sent all the way from Yorkshire to Bristol, to be forwarded by sea to the coast of Cardigan, while ample stores of bows and arrows, bowstrings, arblasts, stone-shot, sulphur and salt-petre were ordered to be held in readiness at Hereford'. Moreover, while Owain was finding it ever more difficult to raise troops and keep them together, there was a rush of heavily armed English nobles and knights to take part in the campaigns of 1407. It was widely believed that this would be the end of Glyndŵr and his rebellion and they wanted to be in at the kill.

That hunted fox was far from being done for, however. It is true that from 1407 onwards Owain had plainly failed to achieve his main purpose. Unless Henry were overwhelmed by some unsuspected danger from another quarter, Owain could do little more than delay inevitable defeat. But final victory for the English armies was still some years away and would be won only after hard fighting. The two key fortresses of Harlech and Aberystwyth remained in Welsh hands and with them control of a large part of western Wales. A most determined onslaught on Aberystwyth in the summer of 1407 by the prince of Wales was beaten off. The Welsh commander of the castle, Rhys Ddu ('the Black'), then entered into negotiations with the English for the surrender of the castle. Owain would not hear of such a course. Leading a strong relief force, he managed to raise the siege and make the English withdraw. For the time being, both castles remained in Welsh hands.

It was no more than a temporary respite; and elsewhere things were going badly. In France, the murder in November 1407 of Louis of Orléans, the French prince most hostile to England, led to the possibility of arranging a truce between the two countries, from which Owain would be excluded. Back in England Owain lost two more valuable allies in February 1408, when the earl of Northumberland and Lord Bardolph were killed at the battle of Bramham Moor. To add to Welsh discomfiture, the winter of 1407–8 was one of the coldest in memory. A sheet of frozen snow lay thick upon the land from before Christmas until nearly the end of March.

How far the winter's rigours may have weakened the Welsh and reduced their will to resist, it is impossible to tell. But during the following summer of 1408, some time between early July and mid-September, the castle of Aberystwyth fell. To complete the disaster, Harlech was taken later in the same year or early in 1409. Captured in this castle were Owain's wife, two daughters and three grand-daughters, and all were taken into captivity in London. Losing Aberystwyth and Harlech was more than a family disaster and a grave military setback; it meant a drastic reduction in Owain's status. He could no longer credibly maintain the role of a ruling prince; he was once more the hunted outlaw, the guerrilla leader on the run.

He had, at least, escaped, and he still had with him his son, Maredudd, and a number of his leading captains. Even in his reduced state, he was not a man to be ignored by the English authorities. On 16 May 1409, at the time of year when he and his men might be expected to take the field, urgent royal letters were sent to the lords of the March. They were ordered to take up residence in Wales and put down rebellion. Owain, they were told, still had some Frenchmen and Scots with him as well as his own men, and he was devastating far and wide. Six months later, when the rebels might be thought to be going into winter quarters, in November 1409, four of the most powerful lords of the north-eastern March were instructed to stop their officers from making truces with the rebels. The presence of two Scots in Caernarfon suggests that, as late as 1410, some sea connection with Scotland was still being maintained and food and supplies, perhaps, being brought in.

In that year, 1410, came Owain's last major effort – a big raid on the Shropshire border. He was defeated and he lost three of his most loyal captains – Rhys Ddu, Philip Scudamore and Rhys ap Tudur, all of whom were executed. After this setback, a Welsh chronicler tells us, Owain 'made no great attack until he disappeared'. His only notable exploit was his capture of the royalist Dafydd Gam in 1412. Yet even now, such was his reputation and so great the fear his name could inspire, that large and costly royal forces had to be kept in north Wales as a safeguard. In 1411, 300 men-at-arms and 600 archers were drafted there for service at a cost of £8,000 for their wages from 9 July 1411 to 7 April 1412. A year later, Owain's old enemy, Henry IV, died and the prince of Wales succeeded him as Henry V. Anxious to wind up all his problems in Wales, the new king offered a pardon to all the Welsh rebels, including Owain, if they agreed to submit. Resolute to the last, Owain refused.

What eventually became of him, no one can certainly say, and detailed examinations in recent years have not finally resolved the issue. After 1415 he disappeared without trace; by 1417, if not sooner, he was undoubtedly dead. There are a number of varying traditions concerning his death and the place of his burial. One suggests that, realizing he was not the triumphant Owain foretold in prophecy, he slipped away to avoid shame and caused his death to be reported. Another tells us that he left his men in Snowdonia and fled to France. One of Iolo Morganwg's more romantic tales has Owain and his warriors sleeping in a cave in Gwent awaiting the call to arms again. More likely than most is the story that he sought refuge with his daughter, Alice, who had married John Scudamore, a squire descended from a well-known border family. They lived in the secluded manor of Monnington Straddel in the Golden Valley. Here, it would be nice to think, the old warrior may have found a few quiet sunset months of peace before being finally buried in the churchyard there.

Three early sources give the date of his death as either 20 or 21 September 1415; and there is no firm evidence to show that he was alive after that date. The mystery surrounding his death may have arisen because those who were in a position to know what had happened to him had taken steps to preserve the secret. They may well have wanted to ensure that his enemies did not know when he had died or what had happened to his body lest they should inflict indignities upon it. Furthermore, they may have wanted to foster the belief that the hero of prophecy was not dead but was biding his time to reappear in triumph. It may be significant that a Welsh chronicle records that in 1415 he went into hiding and adds, 'very many say that he died; the seers maintain that he did not'.

8

Aftermath

At first sight, it looks as if the Rebellion had been nothing but a catastrophe for Wales. All the great hopes of a new-style Welsh State had failed; resistance had been completely crushed. In the process, the economic life of the country had been all but wrecked. The Welsh, like so many other heavily outnumbered rebel guerrillas, had deliberately resorted to 'scorched earth' tactics so as to bring 'all things to waste that the English should not find strength nor resting-place in the country'. Royal troops had retaliated in the same way. Both sides left in their wake devastated towns and countryside. Trade was stagnant; manors and monasteries were in ruinous state; churches, mills and farm buildings had been destroyed, fields ravaged, livestock captured or slaughtered. Large areas were for years half-populated or even untenanted and deserted. For instance, in 1428, a generation after the end of the Rebellion, in the large lordship of Ogmore in south Wales, more than half the tenant land was unoccupied. In north Wales, the borough of Conwy alone had suffered damage to the tune of £16,000. A century later, in 1536–9, when the great antiquary, John Leland, was touring Wales, he recorded ruin after ruin said to have been 'defaced in Henry the Fourth's days by Owen Glendower'. As late as 1567 Bishop Richard Davies gave a harrowing account of the damage inflicted upon the religious and cultural life of Wales as a result of the Rebellion. He described how books and manuscripts had been destroyed in large numbers and bishops' houses, monasteries and churches burnt all over Wales. We must, it is true, be aware of attributing too much of this ruination to the effects of the Rebellion alone. People were very prone to assign to a single spectacular cause, like the Black Death or the Glyndŵr Rebellion, a decline which was really caused by a long and complex process of economic decay and social crisis. Nevertheless, we have to recognize that the Rebellion had caused appalling devastation and misery.

In other ways, too, it had had unhappy consequences. Far from bringing about greater political or legal freedom for the Welsh, it had brought down on their heads the savage penal laws passed by the English Parliament. These remained on the statute book long after the Rebellion was over, though they were not always strictly enforced. The bitter feelings of antagonism which they symbolized also remained alive. English fears and hostility were expressed by the author of the *Libel of English Policye*, written about 1436:

> Beware of Wales, Christ Jesu must us keep
> That it make not our child's child to weep,
> Nor us also, if it go his way
> By unawareness; since that many a day
> Men have been feared of their rebellion . . .
> Look well about, for God wot we have need.

On the other side, Welsh poets freely voiced their indignation and resentment as well as those of their fellow-countrymen and countrywomen. Lewis Glyn Cothi, for example, blazing with anger against the English burgesses of Flint, sang:

> Henceforth will I abjure for good
> Slavish Flint and all its brood.
> May Hell its furnace fires undo,
> Its English folk and piper too.
> My prayer is, may they perish all –
> My curse on them and their children fall.

Nor was it only against the English that Welsh patriotic wrath was directed. The Rebellion left behind it bitter feuds among the Welsh themselves. Those who had been 'out with Owain' viewed with hatred those who had taken the English side, and strife between them was perpetuated for generations. The Rebellion had wrought emotional as well as material havoc. Many Welsh people, sunk in despair, believed that their failures and troubles were God's punishment on them for their wickedness and lack of faith.

Had it all been a misplaced and wasted effort then? Was it at best no more than a useless protest and at worst a sordid piece of medieval banditry masquerading under a cloak of national sentiment? To view Owain and his Rebellion solely in this light would be grossly unjust. Certainly, he waged war in the ferocious and destructive fashion of his age; in this he was no better and no worse than his contemporaries. Admittedly, too, he had high-flying ambitions for himself as the man of destiny come to fulfil the old prophecies. But he was no mere reckless adventurer pursuing his own ends by cynically exploiting his countrymen's deluded dreams of grandeur and bringing down untold misery on their heads in the process. He was inspired by something more than personal disappointment, common greed, private vengeance, or selfish ambition. He fought also for an ideal widely shared by many, though not all, his compatriots. This was the hope of freedom and independence embodied in the prophecies. Those prophecies may appear to us to be strange and unreal, and we now know that much of the 'history' on which they were based was legendary. But to the man or woman in medieval Wales they were genuine enough. They were a way of expressing values of the utmost importance to them. Joan of Arc's 'voices from heaven', odd as they may seem to us, did the same for France. What both were emphasizing in their different ways was a nation's self-respect. Owain's Rebellion stressed the two essential emotions that underlay the prophecies. First, the awareness of the Welsh that they were a separate people with a history and a culture of their own. Second, that as such they were entitled to be treated with dignity and consideration and not as a conquered race of inferior barbarians.

The ideals remained green long after Owain himself was dead. They resound time and again in the Welsh poetry of the fifteenth century. Harsh though the aftermath of the Rebellion might have been, none of the poets blamed Owain. On the contrary, they saw in him the very pattern of their hopes and desires for other Welsh leaders. He had done for Wales what William Wallace and Robert Bruce did for Scotland, Joan of Arc for France, or John Huss for Bohemia. The patriotism he inspired did much to account for a great deal of the growing Welsh support at the end of the century for Henry Tudor. Henry's victory in 1485 and his accession to the English throne seemed to some Welsh people to be Owain's belated triumph. A Welsh chronicler of Tudor times, Ellis Gruffudd, the soldier of Calais, illustrates this point by relating a legend concerning Owain. It tells how the Welsh prince, walking early one morning on the Berwyn Mountains, met the abbot of Valle Crucis. 'You are up betimes, Master Abbot', said Owain. 'Nay, sire', came the answer, 'it is you who have risen too soon – by a century!'

Of Owain's attraction for the men of his own age we have had ample proof. For fifteen years, amid a divided Welsh population, only about one-twelfth that of England and having an even smaller proportion of wealth and resources, he had kept the flame of insurgency alight. It is not very easy to know how he did it, because we really have so little surviving evidence of what kind of man he was. No contemporary portraits of him have come down to us, and all we have is that very shadowy impression from his seal (Plate 2), which may or may not have been designed as a likeness. What can be gleaned of his childhood, education and upbringing is painfully fragmentary. Though a number of poems addressed to him are extant, all were composed before his rebellion broke out. Valuable as they are, their content is largely confined to those stock public virtues which particularly interested the poets. They tell us virtually nothing about his personal appearance or his more individual characteristics. Nor did the results of the archaeological excavations conducted at his former home at Sycharth prove any more rewarding and added nothing significant to our knowledge of his life-style.

Much of what we know about him derives from sources that were in general hostile: royal and official records and the evidence of English chroniclers. The chances of any substantial body of new material concerning him coming to light are distinctly poor. Both his homes were destroyed in savage punitive operations by royal troops seeking to crush opposition. All his sons died childless, leaving no survivors in the male line who might perhaps have been expected to preserve information relating to the family. Most of the evidence relating to unsuccessful rebels tends anyway to be destroyed and only the records of the victors survive. One early source which has been preserved in a Welsh collection (Panton MS 53) reports that Owain's 'cruelty made the people to leave him and his covetousness made his soldiers by degrees to forsake him'. It adds, however, that his 'courage and valour were excellent'. Quite clearly, he must have possessed some remarkable personal magnetism which drew men to him and retained their loyalty. Nothing vindicates his charisma more emphatically, perhaps, than that during all his long years as a rebel he was never betrayed by his own men; not even in the first, or the last, desperate phase, when many a man might have saved his own skin at the price of Owain's. Nor, as far as we know, was there any effort to supplant him. That sway he continued to exercise over the affections of Welshmen for six hundred years, from his own day down to our own.

The bardic tributes were the nearest thing we have to the voice of Welsh public opinion among Owain's contemporaries. Idealized their portrait may have been and certainly not erring on the side of restraint. Even so, it presents an image of the man and his household seen at their most favourable by two of the most eloquent and articulate of his admiring fellow-countrymen. This was Owain the chivalric leader as he appeared to Gruffudd Llwyd:

> Battling in tournament,
> shattering men's bodies and overthrowing a hundred.
> Silence is commanded for him
> as he sits at table at the head of a goodly company.
> He will tolerate no disorder or injustice,
> a companion fit to mingle with earls.

Or here was part of Iolo Goch's cameo of his family and household:

> The best of wives among ladies . . .
> and his children come in pairs,
> a fine nestful of rulers . . .
> Splendid gifts are never lacking,
> neither is there need, nor hunger, nor shame,
> nor ever thirst in Sycharth.

It was a vision of him the fifteenth-century successors to his bards continued to cherish.

Sir John Edward Lloyd suggested, though, that for Tudor and Stuart writers in Wales Owain was 'the unsuccessful rebel, the ill-starred victim of ambition, whose career was eminently fitted to point the moral of the vanity of human aims and desires'. Admittedly, the best-known Tudor historian of Wales, Dr David Powel, dismissed his claims as 'altogether frivolous' and his concept of an independent Wales as a 'fool's paradise'. Nor were later authors like William Wynn of Garthewin or Edward Lhuyd any kinder to 'that most profligate rebel'. But others during the same period were far more sympathetic to Owain and his ideals. Ellis Gruffudd has already been quoted to this effect (p. 85). George Owen of Henllys, in spite of being a loyal Elizabethan subject who utterly deplored rebellion, none the less warmed to Owain. He argued that if others of the nobility and commons 'had been of Owain Glyndŵr's mind and suppressed Henry IV', then the civil wars between Lancaster and York would never have taken place. 'Judge you', he asked, 'if that seeing his lawful prince [Richard II] suppressed . . . would stretch forth to withstand the usurper, whether he were worthy to be registered for a traitor.' For George Owen it was Henry IV and his 'hard and unreasonable laws' who merited condemnation. Henry was also the villain for Charles Edwards, another writer who could not conceal his partiality for Owain in his *Hanes y Ffydd Ddiffuant* ('History of the Unfeigned Faith') (1674). Around the Welsh insurgent leader, he contended, his countrymen had all gathered, 'urging him to fight against the English in the hope of Myrddin's bruts and prophecies to see if they could regain what their ancestors had lost'. Similarly, the celebrated seventeenth-century antiquary, Robert Vaughan, solicitously gathered up early manuscript materials concerning Owain. Knowledge and traditions about him had, therefore, long been carefully and affectionately preserved before Thomas Pennant 'resurrected' him in the eighteenth century and laid the foundations for his modern reputation.

His fame reached its apogee in the heyday of the triumphant Welsh Liberalism of the end of the nine-teenth century; the years of 'Young Wales' in the 1880s and 1890s. Owain Glyndŵr then looked to be the 'morning star' of their hopes, who shone with dazzling brilliance; the very embodiment of their dominant aspirations but born five hundred years too soon. He appeared to have the same principal targets as those at which they themselves were aiming: the champion of an independent Wales ruled by a Welsh Parliament; of an autonomous Welsh church, reformed as well as freed from English tutelage; and of new institutions of higher education dedicated to national ends. In politics, religion and education he could plausibly be depicted as having led the way. Two of the brightest luminaries of 'Young Wales' were themselves to become historians of exceptional calibre and influence. Owen Edwards maintained that central to Owain's greatness was 'his attempt to create out of the disorder . . . a nation with settled institutions and high ideals'; while John Edward Lloyd was to acclaim him as 'the father of modern Welsh nationalism'. Some more recent commentators have been just as attracted by him. Professor Gwyn A. Williams concluded that 'if there is doubt about Welsh consciousness, even Welsh nationalism, before the revolt, there can be none after it, for the Welsh mind is still haunted by its lightning-flash vision of a people that was free'. Dr Gwynfor Evans is convinced that 'to a host of Welsh people [Owain] will never die. His spirit lives on like an unquenchable flame, a symbol of the determin-ation of the Welsh to live as a free nation'. Professor Rees Davies, ablest and most judicious of contemporary historians of medieval Wales, believes that 'the revolt of Owain Glyn Dŵr, whatever else it may have been and whatever other grievances and aspirations it drew upon, was ultimately founded on a vision of national unity and deliverance'. Though there is much that is unknown, and seemingly can never be known, about him, it is impossible to resist his attraction. Perhaps it is partly because much of his personality, achievement, and ultimate fate is, like King Arthur's, wrapped in impenetrable veils of mystery, that he holds so potent an appeal for Welsh people.

But not only for the Welsh; his enemies were also subject to the attraction of his personality. In the heat of battle the English were apt to regard him as a sinister practitioner of the arts of black magic.

> The King had never but tempest foul and rain
> As long as he was aye in Wales ground;
> Rocks and mists, winds and storms, certain
> All men trowed witches it made that stound.

But then in similar circumstances they burnt Joan of Arc as a witch. Traces of a superstitious fear of Owain persist in later generations: Shakespeare in his play *Henry IV*, Part I, depicts him as calling up 'spirits from the vasty deep'. But this greatest of Englishmen goes deeper into the secrets of Owain's power over men. In an age which regarded rebellion against the crown as the worst of crimes, he nevertheless portrays this Welsh outlaw who, for fifteen years, defied two English kings and a dozen English armies, in a highly sympathetic light. He places him in his gallery of heroes of the British history best known to him. In essence his description is remarkably similar to that of Owain's Welsh poetic admirers. With that tribute we may fittingly take our leave of him:

> In faith, he is a worthy gentleman;
> Exceedingly well-read, and profited
> In strange concealments; valiant as a lion
> And wondrous affable, and as bountiful
> As mines of India.

Principal Dates

1405	Tri-partite Indenture signed. French troops land in Milford Haven and advance to Woodbury Hill.
1406	'Pennal policy' agreed upon. French troops withdraw. South-west Wales and Anglesey submit to Henry IV.
1408	Northumberland defeated at Bramham Moor. Fall of Aberystwyth and Harlech castles.
1410	Last great raid defeated.
1415	Owain refuses pardon offered by Henry V.
1415–17	Death of Owain.

Further Reading

A full and up-to-date bibliography is to be found in P. H. Jones (ed.), *A Bibliography of the History of Wales* (microfiche, 1989). The best and most recent survey of the history of medieval Wales is R. R. Davies, *Conquest, Co-existence and Change: Wales, 1063–1415* (1987) which also contains an excellent bibliography.

E. W. M. Balfour-Melville, *James I King of Scots* (1936).

J. M. W. Bean, 'Henry IV and the Percies', *History,* xliv (1959), 212–27.

H. I. Bell, *Dafydd ap Gwilym: Fifty Poems* (1942)

—— 'Translations from the Cywyddwyr', *Transactions of the Honourable Society of Cymmrodorion*, 1940, 221–53; 1942, 130–47.

I. Bowen, *The Statutes of Wales* (1908).

A. G. Bradley, *Owen Glyndwr* (1902) – an older life, but one of considerable charm and value.

J. Davies, *Hanes Cymru* (1990).

J. D. G. Davies, *Owen Glyn Dŵr* (1934) – lively if controversial.

R. R. Davies, 'Colonial Wales', *Past and Present*, 65 (1974), 3–23.

—— 'Owain Glyn Dŵr and the Welsh squirearchy', *Transactions of the Honourable Society of Cymmrodorion*, 1968 ii, 150–69.

—— 'Race relations in post-Conquest Wales', *Transactions of the Honourable Society of Cymmrodorion*, 1974–5, 32–56.

—— *Lordship and Society in the March of Wales, 1282–1400* (1978).

O. M. Edwards, *Wales* (1901).

H. Ellis, *Original Letters illustrative of English History* (2nd ser., 1827) – contains many letters relating to Wales.

G. Evans, *Land of My Fathers* (1974).

J. R. Gabriel, 'Wales and the Avignon papacy', *Archaeologia Cambrensis*, 7th ser., iii (1923), 70–86.

A. E. Goodman, 'Owain Glyndŵr before 1400', *Welsh History Review*, v (1970–1), 67–70.

R. A. Griffiths, 'Some partisans of Owain Glyn Dŵr at Oxford', *Bulletin of the Board of Celtic Studies*, xx (1962–4), 282–92.

—— 'Some secret supporters of Owain Glyn Dŵr', *Bulletin of the Institute of Historical Research*, 37 (1964), 77–100.

—— 'Gentlemen and rebels in later medieval Cardiganshire', *Ceredigion*, v (1964–7), 143–67.

—— 'The Glyn Dŵr Rebellion in north Wales through the eyes of an Englishman', *Bulletin of the Board of Celtic Studies*, xxi (1966–8),151–68.

Rhidian Griffiths, 'Prince Henry, Wales and the Royal Exchequer', *Bulletin of the Board of Celtic Studies*, xxxii (1985), 202–15.

—— 'Prince Henry's war: armies, garrisons and supply during the Glyndŵr Rebellion', *Bulletin of the Board of Celtic Studies*, xxxiv (1987), 165–73.

D. B. Hague and C. Warhurst, 'Excavations at Sycharth castle', *Archaeologia Cambrensis*, cxv (1966),108–27.

F. C. Hingeston, *Royal Letters of Henry IV* (Rolls series, 1860) – contains letters relating to Wales.

E. Humphreys, *The Taliesin Tradition* (1983).

R. I. Jack, 'New light on the early days of Owain Glyn Dŵr', *Bulletin of the Board of Celtic Studies*, xxi (1964–6), 163–6.

—— 'Owain Glyn Dŵr and the lordship of Ruthin', *Welsh History Review*, ii (1964–5), 303–22.

E. F. Jacob, *The Fifteenth Century* (1961).

A. O. H. Jarman, 'Wales and the Council of Constance', *Bulletin of the Board of Celtic Studies*, xliv (1950–2), 220–2.

E. J. Jones, 'Bishop John Trefor of St Asaph', *Journal of the Historical Society of the Church in Wales*, 23 (1968), 36–46.

G. A. Jones, *Owain Glyndŵr* (1962).

R. H. Jones *The Royal Policy of Richard II* (1968).

J. L. Kirby, *Henry IV of England* (1970).

E. A. Lewis, *The Medieval Boroughs of Snowdonia* (1912).

H. Lewis et al. (eds), *Cywyddau Iolo Goch ac Eraill* (1937).

J. E. Lloyd, *Owen Glendower* (1931) – still the classic work on the subject.

T. Matthews, *Welsh Records in Paris* (1910).

M. McKisack, *The Fourteenth Century* (1959).

J. E. Messham, 'The county of Flint and the Rebellion of Owain Glyndŵr . . .' *Flintshire Historical Society Publications*, 23 (1967–8), 1–34.

W. H. Morris, 'Cydweli and the Glyn Dŵr Revolt', *Carmarthenshire Antiquary*, iii (1959–61), 4–16.

R. Nicholson, *Scotland in the later Middle Ages* (1974).

T. Parry, trans. H. I. Bell, *History of Welsh Literature* (1955).

J. R. S. Phillips 'When did Owain Glyn Dŵr die?' *Bulletin of the Board of Celtic Studies*, xxliv (1970–2), 59–77.

T. J. Pierce, *Medieval Welsh Society* (1972).

W. Rees, *South Wales and the March, 1282–1415* (1924).
—— *An Historical Atlas of Wales* (1951).

E. P. Roberts, 'Tŷ pren glân mewn top Bryn Glas', *Transactions Denbighshire History Society*, xxii (1973),12–47.

G. Roberts, 'The Anglesey submissions of 1406', *Bulletin of the Board of Celtic Studies*, xv (1952–4),39–61.
—— *Aspects of Welsh History* (1969).

T. Roberts, '"An ancient fear record": Anglesey adherents of Owain Glyndŵr', *Bulletin of the Board of Celtic Studies*, xxxviii (1991), 129–33.

A. J. Roderick, (ed.), *Wales through the Ages*, i (1959).

J. B. Smith, 'The last phase of the Glyndŵr Rebellion', *Bulletin of the Board of Celtic Studies*, xxii (1966–7), 250–60.

E. M. Thompson, (ed.), *Chronicon de Ade de Usk* (1904).

J. A. Tuck, *Richard II and the English Nobility* (1973).

R. K. Turvey, 'David Perrot: a Pembrokeshire squire in the service of Glyndŵr', *Transactions of the Honourable Society of the Cymmrodorion*, 1990, 65–82.

G. Williams, *The Welsh Church From Conquest to Reformation* (1976).
—— *Religion, Language and Nationality in Wales* (1979).

—— *Recovery, Reorientation and Reformation: Wales, 1415–1642* (1987).

G. A. Williams, *When was Wales?* (1985).

K. Williams-Jones, 'The taking of Conwy Castle 1401', *Transactions of the Caernarfonshire Historical Society*, 39 (1978), 7–43.

J. H. Wylie, *The History of England under Henry IV* (1884).

In recent years the following valuable studies have been published:

R. R. Davies, *The Revolt of Owain Glyn Dŵr* (Oxford University Press, 1995) – this is a book of quite exceptional importance.

R. R. Davies, *Owain Glyn Dŵr: Trwy Ras Duw Tywysog Cymru* (Gwasg y Lolfa, 2002).

E. R. Henken, *National Redeemer: Owain Glyndŵr in Welsh Tradition* (Cardiff, 1996).

G. Hodges, *Owain Glyn Dŵr: The War of Independence in the Welsh Borders* (Logaston, 1995).

Index

BRANCH DATE
WH 11/05